The 10Ks of Personal Branding

Create a Better You

Kaplan Mobray

iUniverse, Inc.
New York Bloomington

The 10Ks of Personal Branding
Create a Better You

iUniverse books may be ordered through booksellers or by contacting:

iUniverse
1663 Liberty Drive
Bloomington, IN 47403
www.iuniverse.com
1-800-Authors (1-800-288-4677)

ISBN: 978-0-595-48481-2 (sc)
ISBN: 978-0-595-71945-7 (hc)
ISBN: 978-0-595-60573-6 (ebook)

Printed in the United States of America

iUniverse rev. date: 1/12/2009

To my loving wife, Astrid, who shows me the beauty of life every day through her smile. Thank you for your support and encouragement in making the 10Ks a reality.

(K)ontents

Acknowledgments ix

The Power of (K) xi

About Me xiii

Introduction xxi

The 10Ks of Personal Branding xxiii

Chapter 1K Know Thyself 1

Chapter 2K Know What You Want to Be Known For 16

Chapter 3K Know How to Be Consistent 32

Chapter 4K Know How to Accept Failure as Part of Building Your Personal Brand 40

Chapter 5K Know How to Communicate Your Personal Brand Attributes 45

Chapter 6K Know How to Create Your Own Opportunities 55

Chapter 7K Know and Master the Art of Connection 70

Chapter 8K Know That Silence is Not an Option 98

Chapter 9K Know Your Expectations (Not Your Limitations) 115

Chapter 10K Know Why You Are Doing What You Are Doing Today and How it Will Shape Where You Are Headed Tomorrow 131

Special K Know How to Ask For What You Want 137

Building Your Brand 145

(K)atchup 185

Acknowledgments

First and foremost I would like to acknowledge the process of writing a book as one of the most humbling experiences that I have had to endure. I have learned some lifelong lessons and have discovered a deeper passion for helping others through sharing one's perspective. There have been many extraordinary people who have played a special role in the development of this book and the life I know as Kaplan Mobray. I would like to thank several of them here.

Thanks to Mark Levit, managing partner of Partners and Levit Advertising and professor of Marketing at New York University who first gave me an opportunity to speak to his students as a guest lecturer on February 15, 2006. It was on that night that I gave birth to the 10Ks of Personal Branding. I will be forever grateful for that opportunity and for you believing in me and the impact this message will have on the world.

To Brian Flynn, former National Marketing Director at Citibank, where I started my professional career. Thanks for getting in that elevator on the 50th floor and listening to my elevator speech. Those six seconds still remain one of the most valuable six seconds I have spent in my life. To Orlando Lima, CEO of social networking site Limachips.com. Thanks for not only years of friendship but for giving me my first online presence to share this inspirational message with the world.

To Ric Cavalcante and Nick Koontz at Innergate Entertainment, thanks for your consultancy and helping me to make the 10Ks message a multimedia product and service.

To Lailo Varsa, you have a gift for making images talk. Thank you for your keen eye as my designer, photographer and 10K creative consultant.

Priscilla Ajao, my former chief of staff and the first 10K disciple. Thanks for living the 10Ks principles every day and letting me know that they make a difference in your life and are helping you to reach your personal and professional goals.

To Barbara Smith, my executive coach from Novations Inc, you gave me the gift of a listening ear to help me find my purpose and the courage to insert wisdom to create possibilities.

To the Association of Latino Professionals in Finance and Accounting (ALPFA), one of the nation's leading professional organizations, and to the number of other professional and student associations who created opportunities for me to share this motivational message with your members. Your efforts are truly making a difference in helping others to better themselves and their professional outcomes. Thank you for making me a part of your formula for success.

To Deloitte LLP, an organization whose commitment to talent and diversity continues to set the standard of excellence in corporate America. I thank the Firm, its leaders, and my colleagues for the support to pursue a personal passion and to make it a reality given the demands of the professional services industry. It is extraordinary leaders like CEO Barry Salzberg, Chief Diversity Officer Allen Thomas, Global HR Leader Jim Wall and Marketing Director Sandra Viola that transform vision into action and enable one's skill to create sustainable results. To these leaders I am appreciative and grateful for your mentorship and support of my career.

The biggest contributor to the success of this effort is the support of my family and all those who I am honored to call friends. Each of you has played a special role in the development of this book and the life experiences that I have treasured along the way. I thank you for your support.

To my wife, Astrid, thank you for your positive encouragement in what was a physically and mentally demanding project. Your belief in me and unwavering support through all the late nights, early mornings, weekends, and travel helped keep me focused.

To my daughter Danse, you were born around the same time as the launch of this book. Your timely entrance into the world gave me an added boost of energy and motivation and greater meaning to everything I do in life. I live to return to you daily the joy that you have brought our family.

To my parents George and Boblin Mobray, thank you for your confidence in me, for instilling pride in my work ethic and for your sacrifice over the years so that I could dream bigger and create the means for those dreams to come true. To my brothers and sisters Deon, Gail, Brian, and Natasha, you are the reason that I continue to pursue excellence. I strive to always be an example and a role model.

And finally, to all who have the courage to live each day as a brand. Thank you for validating the importance of personal branding and the impact it has on creating a better you.

The Power of (K)

Welcome to the 10Ks of Personal Branding—the ultimate guide to understanding how to create, manage, and project your personal brand!

(K)nowledge is power. In this book, (K) represents a universal symbol of knowledge. I define (K) as a state of being, a state of knowing, and the active state of taking something to the next level. The 10Ks represent the knowledge you need to build your personal brand. Each (K) is a prescription that focuses on a specific action, thought, or experience that will help you dramatically transform yourself into a winning brand.

The 10Ks of Personal Branding are:

(K)now Thyself
(K)now What You Want to Be Known For
(K)now How to Be Consistent
(K)now How to Accept Failure As Part of Building Your Personal Brand
(K)now How to Communicate Your Personal Brand Attributes
(K)now How to Create Your Own Opportunities
(K)now And Master the Art of Connection
(K)now That Silence is Not An Option
(K)now Your Expectations (Not Your Limitations)
(K)now Why You Are Doing What You Are Doing Today and How it Will Shape Where You Are Headed Tomorrow

Special K: Know How to Ask For What You Want

About Me

I have long been a student of brands. In my early childhood, I used to watch television commercials and rate which ones would make me buy the product being advertised. I recognize that this behavior was quite odd for a young kid my age, but for some reason I was fascinated by television commercials. It probably explains why my favorite day in school was show and tell. On show and tell day, I would draw pictures of my favorite superheroes and products I had seen on TV and bring them in to show the class. As my habit for watching commercials grew, I developed a strong memory for logos. At age ten I could recall eighty percent of the slogans and jingles I saw on television. At that time my favorite commercials were for Coca-Cola, McDonalds, and Jell-O. If you poll most kids seven and under today, it would be interesting to see what commercials they remember and if they have the same list.

Fast forward several years later. My passion for brands led me to study marketing management while attending the University of Pennsylvania Wharton School of Business. At college I had an internship as a sales representative with Procter & Gamble, an experience that would cement my appreciation for the power of a brand.

I was eighteen years old and responsible for a sales territory of thirty-five grocery stores. During this internship I sold personal care products like shampoo, deodorant, facial cream, and toothpaste. This experience introduced me to the concepts of product brands, packaging, promotion, price, and people: what some call the 5Ps. Each day I would wake up, put on a navy blue suit, a sharply-pressed white shirt, and a red tie, and walk into a grocery store with eight cartons of health and beauty care products I hoped to sell.

Being a sales representative was an exciting job but came with its share of challenges. During the course of my internship, my goal was to sell one thousand cartons of health and beauty care products and distribute them among thirty-three grocery stores throughout northeast Philadelphia. This was a lofty goal for an intern, but one that I took on with an eagerness to prove myself.

The first few weeks were tough. I visited ten stores and walked away with zero sales. I knew I represented the best products in the category, and had the best aisle placement on the shelves; however there was something that was preventing me from convincing the store managers to buy more products.

I developed a basic formula for my sales presentation:

1. A welcome greeting
2. Use seasonal trends in consumer shopping behavior to highlight a consumer issue
3. Indicate how the product benefits would solve the consumer issue
4. Talk about the product features
5. Ask about product inventory levels
6. State the price value of the product
7. Close the sale

I organized my presentation this way to ensure that I could share as much information on the product as possible without taking up too much of the store manager's time. For some reason, however, it was not working.

In high school I was a varsity athlete and was accustomed to competing as a runner and winning games as a basketball star. I knew what it meant to lose a game because I missed a shot, but for some reason this type of rejection felt different. I internalized it deeply. During the next several months I worked hard on my sales pitch. At nights I would practice before a mirror and spend time researching sales techniques on the Internet so that I could refine the way I introduced myself to the store managers each day. I also watched how other sales reps entered the store to see if I could pick up any tips to make me better at selling. After much reflection, I was ready to try a new approach. I decided for the next few weeks instead of walking into the store and following a script, I would greet every store manager with a smile that was accompanied by a "quote of the day."

Sometimes I would find quotes from the tea bags that I used each morning or from the Snapple bottle caps I drank for lunch. Other times I would make them up and try to find a quote that could bring a smile, laughter, or hope, depending on my audience. This tactic was a bit of a surprise for the store managers on my route. They had been used to seeing me come into their store with two fifteen pound boxes full of products and could anticipate what I was going to say. But for my new sales approach I left the cartons in my car and entered the store with my hands free. I started my greeting with a new formula:

1. A welcome greeting
2. Ask about their weekend or how their morning was going
3. Explain how my morning was going or details of how I spent my weekend
4. Share a quote of the day to help them get through the morning
5. Ask about how they were doing with product inventory levels
6. Let them know if they needed more products I could supply them with two extra cartons at the seasonal price
7. Close the sale

In the first version of my sales approach I focused ninety percent of my conversation on the product that I was trying to sell and the remaining ten percent on the connection with the store manager. Using my new sales approach, I focused ninety percent of my time on the connection with the store manager and ten percent on the product sales pitch. A couple of weeks went by and soon my rejection rate had decreased. I was now successfully selling into ten out of every twelve stores I visited, and in some stores the managers eagerly waited for the morning quote so they could share it with their associates.

The summer went by quickly. At the end of my internship I had sold twelve hundred cartons, raised one hundred and twenty thousand dollars in new product sales, and grew my territory by thirty percent over the previous summer's intern. More than the value of any sale, however, I had earned the respect of the thirty-five store managers in my territory who had initially dismissed me at the start of my internship.

Lessons Learned

There were many lessons I learned that summer, but none were more apparent than the importance of having a personal brand. I learned that you cannot sell a product without first creating an experience or environment where people buy into you. In other words, the most important brand that you can sell is "you."

With my quote of the day, I created an experience that established a connection with the store managers. At the same time, I differentiated myself from the other sales reps. In essence, I became my own brand. This enabled me to get more face time with the store managers, build stronger relationships, and sell more products.

My summer internship at Procter & Gamble encouraged me to continue to study brands. I embarked on a customized focus for my career at the University of Pennsylvania combining sociology, the study of people, with marketing, the study of brands. At the start of my senior year and the critical job search process, I spoke to advertising agency account directors, brand managers at consumer product companies, and marketing executives at financial institutions to gain more information on how I could apply this discipline in the business world. Several months went by and I must have had over forty interviews with various people at companies from Pittsburgh to San Francisco. That fall I felt like a political candidate, traveling from state to state trying to secure a vote of confidence and employment.

I ultimately landed a job in New York, starting my career at Citibank as a marketing manager in their management associate program. I can remember my interviews leading up to my offer quite vividly. The interviewer asked me about my qualifications and why I was pursuing a career in marketing at a bank. For each interview I had a slogan, "The better you understand people, the better your ability to help a company sell products to them." I explained that banks offer products to consumers and that the concept of selling a checking account was no different than selling hamburgers to hungry consumers. I went on to explain that a bank branch is no different from a fast food restaurant. In one of my interviews I offered a suggestion to bring attention to the company's brand. I suggested they call it "McBank." After my interviews word soon spread of the humorous slogan and caught the ears of several executives who immediately wanted to know who I was.

I thought at that moment that I definitely had lost the job, and blown the interview. The head of the New York office requested that I meet with him before leaving. I walked into his office expecting him to admonish me for using the company's brand name as a joke and tell me I didn't have the job. I was prepared to be fired before even getting hired for the job. To my surprise, he shook my hand and said, "Pleasure to meet you. That was a funny slogan. McBank, very funny! Have a nice day."

I walked out of his office not knowing if I had committed ultimate interview suicide or if I just made him laugh. Later that night I got a call from the recruiter. "Kaplan, congratulations! I am pleased to inform you that we would like to offer you a job in our Management Associate program working with our marketing group." I was thrilled and relieved at the same time. After a few moments, when the reality of what I had achieved set in, I had a brief flashback to my internship days at Procter & Gamble. I remembered sharing the quotes each morning with the store managers and thought about how the slogan "McBank" may have helped me get the job. I must admit; at the time I did not realize how much of a risk I took in attempting to be different.

Five years later I was recruited by a large advertising agency and eventually left Citibank for Madison Avenue to lead account management activities for a high profile pharmaceutical company. As an account supervisor at Deutsch advertising I learned how to build a brand from the ground up. My training gave me an understanding of how to organically take a brand's attributes and package them to create consumer appeal and drive sales. My favorite part of coming to work was working with what they call "the creatives." These were the people who drew the pretty pictures, wrote the slogans that made brands come to life, and sometimes had red, green, pink, and blue hair. The inner creative in me came out, and before long I began adding phrases to slogans and providing input to shape the creative design of ads. I even had a thought about putting some color in my hair!

When I look back on those years building my career, I reflect on the fact that my childhood love for watching TV commercials had evolved to now developing them for big companies. My single greatest joy was to come home from work and see the commercial I had helped develop at work months ago appear on television that night. I took pride in saying to my friends, "I worked on that commercial." It humbly brought me back to my early days of watching TV as a kid.

In June of 2000 I was downsized from my job at the ad agency and my life changed. For the first time I had no answer to the question, "Who are you and what do you do?" Living in New York City and not having answers to these questions was like being without an ID when you just turned 21. I was out of work for three months, and although it was a difficult time for me under the circumstances, this life change proved to be the turning point in my life.

Life Change

I remember one day while attending a networking event with a friend, someone approached me and asked, "What do you do for a living?" This was the moment I had dreaded.

I took a deep breath, smiled confidently, looked the person in the eye, and said, "I am Kaplan Mobray and I inspire others."

When I think back to that moment, I realize that it was one of the first times where I did not define myself by something I physically or materially possessed. I had lost my job, my bank account was steadily depleting, and I had recently ended a long-term relationship. Other than the support of my family and friends, I had reached a rather low point. What changed for me in that moment was that I found my personal brand: "Inspire." I was able to confidently define myself by the impact I wanted to have on others and not by a job title or possession.

The person looked back at me with some astonishment. My unique response led to a conversation where we discussed my educational background, my professional experiences, and my outlook on life. Our dialogue continued and it facilitated several introductions to other professionals that night who listened to my story and examples of how I helped transform the brands of major companies during my professional career.

Weeks later, one of the contacts I met that night put me in touch with a friend who invited me to interview with her company for a senior marketing position. After three rounds of interviews I was offered a job as a national marketing manager for one of the company's largest divisions. This was a humbling moment given all that I had endured during the previous months. It was especially meaningful because in each of the interviews I had to brand myself to convey value, even though I was unemployed and competing against candidates who had more experience in the industry. For each of the interviews I went in with a formula for how I would brand myself. I gave myself three adjectives I would seek to convey in the interview: creative professional, differentiated outlook, inspire internal employees. I knew that the safe and obvious choice would be to take someone who had worked for a competitor and had more relevant experience. After all, I had come from a totally different industry with no relevant experience, so I represented the most risk of all the candidates. I branded myself as "the outsider looking in" and "the one who could bring a different perspective." In each of the interviews I shared how my background and knowledge of marketing and advertising from another industry could be a valuable asset in helping the company to distinguish its marketing efforts. I explained that I would bring fresh ideas, an outside perspective on how to communicate with clients, and could help the organization inspire its employees through the development of creative communications. So in essence I branded myself before I entered the interviews and had a clear focus on the strengths that I would convey and how they could position me to land the job.

I often refer back to this time in my life and the lessons I learned about the importance of having a personal brand. It helped me to realize that the value you place on your self-worth will influence the value that others place on your current and future capabilities. I learned that if you know yourself well it will convey confidence. Walking into grocery stores as a sales intern and sharing a quote each morning taught me that if you are consistent at something it will create a strong impression. My early rejection from the store managers taught me that it is okay to fail as long as you accept your failures as tools to make you better. As a result of the networking encounter during those three months when I was unemployed, I learned that the way you communicate who you are is just as important as who you claim to be. I also learned that sometimes you have to create your own opportunities and build on the impressions you leave with others.

Further, I realized the importance of establishing a meaningful connection with others as a way to do business. My experiences in the McBank interview taught me that sometimes you have to speak up and use creativity to differentiate yourself. I also learned that if you limit yourself from achieving your expectations, others will limit the scope of your capabilities. And finally, as a kid who grew up watching television commercials, I learned that the things we do today have a direct connection to who we become tomorrow, and if you recognize this early on, you will live your dreams every day.

These experiences gave me the foundation from which I developed the 10Ks of Personal Branding. I share this personal story not to highlight my professional accomplishments but to emphasize the impact that a well-defined personal brand can have on your life and your career.

When I look back on that night at the networking event, the outcome could easily have been different. When asked, so what do you do? I could have replied, "I am unemployed, a little down on my luck, and just trying to recover from being downsized." I am most certain that had I given this response I would have not made the same impression with the contacts I met that night and would not have gained access to the same opportunities that I was later able to achieve.

Your personal brand is not about what you have materially but about how you view yourself. This ultimately shapes how you are viewed by others.

Having a personal brand is power, it builds confidence, makes your life better, and your career more fulfilled. I have long been a student of brands, but over the course of my life I realize the most important commercial you can create is the one about you. I want to help you develop your personal brand so you too will have the power to be the best version of yourself you can be.

Introduction

Have you ever wondered why some people get ahead and others don't? If you are like most people you think about this often and devote your life working to achieve success, greatness, focus, wealth, power, respect, fulfillment, and many of the other buzz words that have dominated the self-help section of bookstores.

My parents always wanted each of their five children to succeed and have a better life than they did, but they too wondered how they could create the foundation for success when growing up poor the only s-word we knew was survival. Get-rich schemes were replaced with "get-by," "know-how" meant "no-choice," and twenty-four hours meant two twelve-hour shifts at work. Growing up, I was told to work hard, study hard, get good grades, go to college, and you can get a good job. You may have heard this too or continue to hear it today. I like to refer to this mantra as the national anthem of the American dream. "Work hard, study hard, get good grades, go to college, and get a good job, bingo! You have success!

I admit, I sang this national anthem many times. During the course of my career I worked hard, studied hard, got good grades, and did get some great jobs. In the process I realized that a good job is no guarantee of success. Furthermore, even if you gain requisite skills as a student, a worker, or a professional, there is no guarantee that you are considered in today's terms a "talent." I learned that success and advancement has just as much to do with how you are perceived as it does what you accomplish and the earlier you understand this, the greater your chance of truly becoming successful.

That's why I created this book; my objective is to help you become a better version of yourself so you can realize more positive outcomes in your personal journey to success.

Great Brands

If you think about the great brands of the world today, one thing they all have in common is the ability to create an expectation of quality, superior benefits, and a defining experience. More importantly, they do this in a quick and consistent manner. Good brands are able to establish a quick association of positive attributes that influence a desired behavior or action. But what about your brand? Do you establish a quick association of positive attributes with those you encounter? Furthermore, are you able to influence a desired behavior or action in your favor based on who you are perceived to be?

The fact is, when you view yourself as a brand you are more capable of managing specific behaviors and actions that drive how people perceive you. That's what personal branding is all about. Think about when you go shopping. The products you select to fill your cart are the ones you trust. Your purchase decisions are based on a preconceived expectation of quality, a great price, a well-known brand, or a product that was referred to you by a friend. Similarly, people select you based on a preconceived expectation of what you will deliver. The greater your ability to use your personal attributes to brand yourself to an expectation of something positive, the more likely you are to drive successful outcomes for your life and career.

People who are successful manage their life toward a concrete outcome

Success has just as much to do with how you are perceived as it does with what you accomplish

A good job is no guarantee of success

There is a difference between skill and talent

The 10Ks of Personal Branding

What Does Success Look Like?

People who are successful manage their life toward a concrete outcome. In other words, they set goals and don't wait for things to happen, they make things happen. They don't accept no for an answer, they create a plan to see possibilities. They are not afraid to look into the mirror, and they always ask themselves the tough questions first. Having a focus on concrete outcomes means having a specific objective you want to accomplish, with a specific time frame for when you want to achieve it, and a specific measure of your success.

Success is about the mirror you look into each morning and how you use the reflection you see to shape the life you live. I call this personal branding. So let's get ready for what will be a life altering experience. My goal is to inspire you to dramatically change the business of your life. If you lack focus you will find it. If you seek empowerment you will harness it. And if you just want to know how to use your personal brand to begin living a better version of you, I will give you the tools to start living it. Welcome to the 10Ks of Personal Branding.

Instructions

For best results, you will need the following ingredients:

- One pen or pencil
- One bag of chocolate candy (any kind) or preferred treat
- One quiet area to reflect on your life
- One friend or colleague who will commit to giving you feedback
- One mirror to see yourself as you always wanted to be

Please note: You will experience a certain level of repetition while embarking on this journey. It is by design and intended to solidify the definition of your personal brand. Please fasten your seatbelts as we are about to begin.

The Tough Questions

Okay, let's get started by taking an inside view of your true self. For each question below, write down the first thing that comes to mind. Take no longer than ten seconds to complete your answer. These thoughts will come in handy later.

- Who are you?____________________________________
- Who do you want to be?____________________________
- Are they the same people?__________________________
- How do you see yourself?___________________________
- How do others see you?____________________________
- When you look into the mirror, is there a difference between how you think you are perceived and how others actually see you?
____
- Does the perception that others have of you help or prevent you from achieving your life goals?__________________________
- What are your life goals?___________________________
- What is your life plan?_____________________________
- How do you deal with failure?_________________________
- What is the one adjective people use most when describing you?
____
- What is the adjective you use most when you describe yourself?
____

Think for a second. What if you could manage the way others perceive you? What if you could do this and learn impression management as a skill to dramatically improve your life?

The reality is that there is a clear connection between your personal view of yourself, the personal view others have of you, and the outcomes you experience in life. The key is to manage this equation so you are projecting outwardly the "you" you know you are, or the "you" you want to become. I call this personal branding. Personal branding is not about grooming and hygiene as many have come to think and write about. It goes far beyond anything you do to your external self and starts with an outlook you develop from within. Many authors have written about the importance of having a personal brand. They describe personal branding as an activity that highlights one's external appearance and grooming, attitude, and reputation. Several have also suggested personal branding is something you do by having a business card, using Google search optimization to make your name or company top the list of searchable items, or placing your business logo in unconventional mediums. Many also go on to advocate the use of blogs as a means to build your personal brand. While I agree that these tools are essential to help gain exposure, they do not provide a how-to method for developing a personal brand.

Whether you are a business owner or a person just simply looking to achieve happiness and life fulfillment, personal branding is for you. The difference in what you are about to read and the other opinions on personal branding is that I have provided a how-to manual for getting in touch with your true self and managing yourself as a world-class brand. You cannot build a personal brand without first understanding you, the person. The 10Ks will give you a blueprint to put you, the person, in context with you, the brand.

When managed well, your personal brand will help you to create more favorable outcomes for your life and will have a dramatic effect on your career success. I've developed a formula that will guide you to an understanding of your personal brand and how to manage it. I call it The 10Ks of Personal Branding.

Thank you for taking the time to read to this point. I encourage you to be an active participant in the experience of this book and assure you that you will walk away with the tools to create a better you.

Chapter 1K

Know Thyself

In This Chapter

- Learn to know yourself
- Define personal qualities, such as strengths and weaknesses
- Personal branding defined
- Create "about me" card statements
- Connect facets of life to create opportunities and achieve goals (GUESS work and ACCESS)

Knowing others is intelligence; knowing yourself is true wisdom. Mastering others is strength; mastering yourself is true power.

-Tao Te Ching

How Well Do You Know Yourself?

The first and primary element in developing a personal brand is having an intimate knowledge of yourself. To do this you must have a complete understanding of who you are, what you believe in, what you stand for, what makes you unique, and what you are most passionate about. This inside view will help you to tap into the true power that gives you your sense of self and the personal component of your brand.

To help us get started, let's answer some fundamental questions about you.

1. What are three words that describe your strengths?____________
   ____________ ____________

2. What are three words that describe your weaknesses? ___________ ___________ ___________

3. What is one thing about yourself that makes you different than those around you? ___________________________

4. In a crowded room, what would make you stand out? ___________ ___________________________

5. What is it that makes you unique within an organization or group? ___________________________

Your answers to these questions will help you assess your internal and external attributes that provide the ingredients to create your personal brand. They will also help you to understand the basis that others use to "choose you," "refer you," "select you," and "hire you" to be on their team.

Getting Comfortable in Your Own Skin

People want to be around people who are comfortable in their own skin. When you know what makes you different you can project your uniqueness with confidence. Your strengths are assets that help you promote your capabilities. Your weaknesses give you a blueprint for self-improvement. The characteristics that make you unique give you a value proposition to overcome competition. Still, many of us struggle with a true acceptance of who we are and avoid personal branding because we are uncomfortable talking about ourselves.

So why is it easier to talk about others than it is to talk about ourselves? The fact is we spend much more time focusing on the brands we consume as a part of everyday living than on our own personal brand. In doing so, we often live our life and build our careers by passive default and not active decision. Thus, it takes us longer to get where we really want to go in life, even assuming we know where we are headed.

If you had to record a thirty second commercial on yourself, what would you say? What would be your hook? Your story line? Your jingle? What would you sell?

Our Greatest Fear

For most of us the thought of giving a public announcement is among our top ten fears. In 1973, *The Book of Lists* by David Wallechinsky, Irving Wallace, and Amy Wallace included a study that cited public speaking as the number one fear in life, well ahead of death. The average person would rather jump out of an airplane, spend a month in prison, or undergo dental surgery than give a formal presentation. As many comedians have said, we as humans would rather be the person lying in the coffin than the one giving the eulogy.

Unfortunately, whether we like it or not, we give a public announcement of our self everyday. The Newspaper Association of America reports that the average person sees well over three thousand advertising messages a day:

> Not too long ago, the average American was exposed to over three thousand advertising messages in the average day. Today, you get that many before breakfast! Everyone is trying to build a brand. This season, the networks have added one more minute of commercials per half-hour, and that is just the beginning. Have you seen the ads in golf holes (talk about hidden persuaders), in bathroom stalls, on grocery register receipts and even in the sand on the beach?[1]

If you hold this logic to be true, then as a personal brand you too are giving over three thousand public announcements each day just by creating an impression and responding to the messages you receive. With all this training, you should have an intimate knowledge of who you are, what makes you different, and how to publicly address an audience on the topic of you. For many of us, however, we do not know how to answer this question. As you think it, are you aware of the over three thousand messages you are sending each day? And do you really understand what those messages are conveying about your brand? As I mentioned, the majority of us spend much more time focusing on other brands than on our own personal brand.

Image is Everything

If you have ever bought a car, think about how much time you put into that purchase. Every decision, right down to the interior detail, is made based on an image you want to convey to others through the purchase of the car. For some, this may be an eight-month process complete with researching the vehicle online, test driving a particular make and model, asking friends' opinion of the car, and looking at advertisements in the newspaper. For others, it takes years of building an affinity to a certain make and model before making a final purchase.

Several psychology journals support the fact that consumers make purchase decisions based on image. An article by Jane Spear in *The Gale Encyclopedia of Psychology* notes, "The key to unlocking consumer psychology is understanding that desires rule over needs when it comes to consumer purchase."[2] The article further cites image and symbolism as one of four factors that influence a consumer's purchase actions. From product spokespersons to the picture on a candy bar wrapper, the ever-elusive association people make with a product might be a big factor in whether or not they buy it, more than the nature or quality of the product itself.

As consumers we buy products and build an affinity to brands based on what the products or brands say about us. But how much time do you spend building an affinity to yourself so that others can buy into you? If you are like most people, the attention you pay to decisions on other brands far outweigh the focus on your personal brand.

As a result, you may be missing out on opportunities and slowing the timeline for you to achieve success. Building a strong personal brand will help you reach your life goals by giving you tools to create greater focus to get where you want to go in life.

Life is a series of increments of now.

Paste this quote on your refrigerator or a place where you can see it at the start of every day. It will help you to focus on living the moments of your now and remind you that the path to your dreams begins by living each step of the journey.

Personal Branding Defined

At the start of this chapter I stated that the first and primary element in developing your personal brand is having an intimate knowledge of yourself. But what is personal branding? Really? And why all the hype and attention to this topic? Let me explain this concept further and help shed some light on why it is a topic we will be talking about for the years to come. I define personal branding as:

The ability to deliberately use attributes that demonstrate your capability to manage the expectations one will receive from an encounter with you.

Let's dissect this definition. There are some key words that will help you understand personal branding as a concept and assess what it means for you. Each of the following questions represent another way to better evaluate how well you know yourself and give you a foundation for how well others will come to know you. Let's start with the word **deliberate.**

What in your life have you been most deliberate about? Is it your family, your career, achieving success, work-life balance, work-work balance, personal finances, finding a mate, finding a job, getting a degree, pursuing a dream? Write your answers to these questions on the lines below.

Question One
What in your life have you been most deliberate about?

____

____

____

____

Question Two
What has been the outcome of your deliberate focus?

____

____

____

____

Please write your answers down throughout this book; they will be a great source of reflection. Trust me; you will want to come back to them later. As you begin to better understand your personal brand, you will find that your responses will change or the questions will become easier to answer.

When you focus, the picture for achieving results becomes clearer.

The second key word in this definition is **attributes.** In other words, the sum of personal traits, inner qualities, style, and adjectives you use to describe yourself.

Question Three
What are some of the words you use to describe yourself?

The next key word is **capability.**

Question Four
What are you capable of? Who are you capable of becoming? In other words, what are you not doing with your life right now that you know you are capable of achieving?

And the final set of words: **manage expectations**.

Question Five
On a day-to-day basis, how do you manage the expectations others have of you? Is it the way you dress, the people who comprise your network, your occupation, your title, your working style, your responsiveness, your actions, your reputation?

Having a true understanding of this technical definition of personal branding will help simplify what it means to you. Let's go back to those five key words: deliberate, attributes, capability, manage expectations. If I were to simplify this, I could come up with a few statements to interpret the definition.

1. Deliberate attributes are capable of managing expectations
2. The capability to manage expectations comes from deliberate actions

3. You can set expectations by deliberately managing your personal attributes as a distinct capability

However you translate it, just know that personal branding is for you, about you, and is something you should not live without.

Your Personal Brand Commitment

Before you read on, close your eyes and take the next five seconds to make a commitment to change your life.

Welcome back! If you have decided to read on, congratulations! You have made a conscious choice to change your life and to begin living as a personal brand. Now let's put this commitment in writing.

10K Branding Change My Life Agreement

On this ____ day of ____ in the year____ I make a commitment to change my life. I will start living to attain the goals I want for my life and career. I will focus on branding myself so others see what I want them to know about me and my capabilities. I will use the 10Ks of Personal Branding principles to help me on this journey. I am committed to achieving great results.

____

Signature   Date

The agreement you just signed confirms your pledge to live a "better" and more fulfilled life. The principles that you are about to explore are principles that I live by and have shaped the lives of many others I have counseled on living as a brand. Take them with you wherever you go. Take them home, take them to school, to your job, take them with you on vacation, and share them with your friends. Just don't leave them trapped in this book. I want this book to help you transform yourself from a perception into a new reality, so that you can start living your personal life and managing your career with a focus on positive outcomes. It all starts with your personal brand.

Your "About Me" Card

Do you have a personal and professional statement of your value? Today, we all carry with us some form of identification. Look in your wallet. I bet you have an identification card, a driver's license, a passport, a work ID, a credit or debit card, or some other documentation that states who you are and confirms what you are worth. Many of us carry these items with us every day but still walk around without a clue on how to communicate our personal value. So if you think about it, many of us struggle to identify ourselves without these cards. If this is you, you are not alone.

The one card that most of us do not carry with us is the "about me" card. The "about me" card is a ready-to-use statement of your value that you can use at over three-hundred encounters with others daily. It is widely accepted and will give you access to opportunities without a swipe. There is no magnetic strip, but it delivers information in a quick and consistent manner to help others buy into you. This is the card you don't want to leave home without.

Creating Your "About Me" Card

The three most common ways that people brand themselves are through:

1. Personal hobbies or activities
2. Job, occupation, or career interests
3. Relationships with others

Because of this I have created three "about me" card statements. Each provides a quick way to brand yourself in the context of the situation in which your personal brand will be displayed. So let's add one more thing to your wallet and create your "about me" card statements.

Example One: Branding Yourself Through Your Personal Hobbies and Interests

I am (*insert your name here)*______________________________,

In my personal time I enjoy *(insert your passion, hobbies, or interests here)* __________________________________. The lessons I have learned from these personal interests have given me three skills I use in my life and bring to my workplace. They include:

Skill Number One: ______________________

Skill Number Two:______________________

Skill Number Three:______________________

Now write your complete "about me" personal attributes statement on the lines below:

____

____

____

Example Two: Branding Yourself Through Your Job, Occupation, or Career Interests

I am (*insert your name here)*________________________

I am a (insert your occupation, job title, position, here_______ _______________.

I have a passion for *(insert what you are known for or principles you are driven by here)*________________. My background doing *(insert your career background and/or life experiences here)*______ ___________, make me a unique individual within *(insert your company name, job department, personal, or desired area of interest here)* ___________.

Now write your complete "about me" professional statement on the lines below:

____

____

____

Example Three: Branding Yourself Through Your Reputation and Relationships

I am *(Insert your name here)*__________________________

> My life is driven by *(insert words that describe the driving force(s) in your life*_________________. Whether you know me as *(insert how others know or come in contact with you)*______________ ____________________________________. I want you to take away *(insert what you want others to take away from an encounter with you)* _________________ from that encounter.
>
> Now write your complete "about me" reputation statement on the lines below:
>
> ____
>
> ____
>
> ____

Great job! You have just completed the application for your "about me" card. These personal statements will help you articulate the elements of your personal brand that comprise your life purpose. They will also serve as a guide to direct the impressions you want to leave with others regardless of the context of your encounter.

To illustrate this let's take a look at my three paragraphs:

Example One: I'm Kaplan Mobray. I am a professional saxophone player, author, and motivational speaker. The lessons I have learned from these personal interests have given me three skills that I use in my life and bring to my career and work environment.

- Creativity
- Confidence
- The ability to inspire others to find their best self

Example Two: I'm Kaplan Mobray. I am a marketing and HR executive. I have a passion for creativity, and producing quality results. My experience at both large corporations managing integrated marketing communications and at creative advertising agencies launching brand campaigns, make me a unique individual within corporate marketing departments. My experience leading organizational change in diversity enables me to directly impact the lives of others by creating access to equal opportunity and programs to help people advance in their careers.

Example Three: I'm Kaplan Mobray. My life is driven by passion, a relentless pursuit of success, and a spirit of creativity in everything I do. Whether you know me as an executive, a professional saxophone player, a motivational speaker, an athlete, an author, a salsa dancer, a friend, or a life coach, I want you to be inspired from that encounter to become something great.

These are my three statements. I refer to them daily as a reminder of who I am, what I am capable of achieving, and how I can help others. This is my "about me" card, and it's in my wallet. It helps me to focus each day and allows me to live by a decision I make to live to my brand. What's in your wallet?

Daily "Me" Time

After you have completed your three "about me" card statements, start to refer to them daily. It may seem like a useless task at first, and you may question why you need to read about yourself when you already know who you are. The key when using these three statements is to focus not only on reading the words you use to describe yourself but on assessing how you will live them as a part of your day.

I equate it to getting up in the morning and reading your favorite newspaper or viewing your favorite morning news show. Think about when you get up in the morning, or what you do on your morning commute. You focus on the news each morning because your awareness of the news and current events helps you to focus on how you will live your day. The weather directs what you will wear, sports gives you conversation starters for the early morning buzz, business news helps you understand the market and economic environment that may impact how you spend or invest money, and current events keeps you knowledgeable on the happenings around town. Your daily mastery of these news items creates a perception with others that you are "in the know." It also may be the reason why others come to you first for your opinion on a range of issues. Having this kind of credibility will almost always create positive opportunities and a positive reception. It's the same philosophy with your "about me" statements. Daily focus will drive you to be more in the know about yourself and how you impact others creating positive association for how people perceive you and your personal brand.

You may not be a living example of how you want to live your life today, but you can start to live the life you want to live by having the focus that comes from these personal statements. The other reason for a well-defined "about me" statement is to help you remove the guesswork from your life activities and begin to create more access to the outcomes you desire for your life and career. Let's explore these two concepts further.

Accessing Your Guess Work

I define "GUESS" Work as Growth from Undefined Experiences, Skills, and Schooling. Essentially it is the sum of past experiences and skills that you have acquired to get you to this point in your life and career. For many of us, this list of experiences is not something we have formally defined for ourselves as a key element of our brand. When you are able to define the elements of your past experiences you are able to frame them as a part of who you are and in doing so become more aware of the rationale behind the choices you have made along the way. Once you are aware of the choices you have made and specifically what they say about you, you can then better connect them to your ultimate life and career goals.

I define **"ACCESS"** as Actions, Choices, Contacts, Experiences, Skills, and Schooling. Achieving your life and career goals takes focus. More importantly, it requires action. You must make specific choices to create a working plan that connects your past experiences, the inventory of your skills, and the resources in your personal or professional network with the steps you must take to achieve your goals. Let's explore this further. Please answer the following four questions below:

1. What do you aspire to be in life or your career?

____

____

____

____

2. What are you doing right now in your life or career?
(Current job, family status, personal pursuits, projects, etc.)

____

____

____

____

3. What training or preparation have you had in the past? (Schooling, degrees, certificates, acquired skills, experience, etc.)

____

____

____

____

4. What training, preparation, or contacts will you need in the future to be what you aspire to be in your life or career?
(Schooling, degrees, certificates, acquired skills, experiences, etc.)

____

____

____

____

Questions one and two are designed to make you reflect on your personal and professional aspirations and help you assess how close you are to obtaining them based on what you are doing today. Let's look at your responses to question number three. Your responses to question number three I call "GUESS" Work.

Now let's look at your responses to question number four. I call your responses to question number four "ACCESS."

As you look at your responses, ask yourself if your life or career is made up of "GUESS" Work; a random sampling of unrelated skills, schooling, and life experiences?

Or, are you gaining "ACCESS" to the things to which you aspire?

The key to "ACCESS" is taking actions and making choices that connect your experiences, skills, schooling, and personal and professional contacts to create the opportunities to achieve your ultimate life goals.

Your personal brand serves as a guide to direct your actions and choices. The key is to know yourself enough to assess if you are making the right decisions. Take a look at what you just wrote for the previous questions one through four. Do you have very different responses across each line? Reflect a moment on your responses and start thinking about the responses that are related to each other. Also reflect a moment on the reasons behind your responses that do not connect. What you may find is that your experiences, skills, and schooling in many cases preceded your understanding of your personal brand. And if this is true, you may have very different or unrelated responses to each question. For example, here's a common "GUESS" Work and "ACCESS" statement I see in many of my workshops:

Sample responses

What do you aspire to be?
"A millionaire, financially secure"

What are you doing right now?

"Working a nine to five job forty hours a week that does not pay enough for what I aspire to be. Working in an occupation that I have to work twenty more years to become financially secure."

What education, training, and preparation have you had in the past?
"High school diploma, college degree, masters degree, previous occupation."

What training, preparation, and contacts will you need in the future to achieve what you aspire to be?

"Need help of a good headhunter. Will need to change jobs or enter new profession, start my own business, go back to school to get my MBA, win the lotto."

So let's look at what training, preparation or contacts you will need in the future to be what you aspire to be. There's a quote from George Elliott that says "It's never too late to be who you might have been." What aspirations have you been holding onto without much success or progress? And why not start now to address your goals head on? The objective here is to remove the "GUESS" work from the sum of your life's activities to create the "ACCESS" that connects what you're doing right now to what you aspire to be. This outlook will give you greater focus to connect how you live to what you want out of life.

By completing your responses to questions one through four, you have conducted an audit of yourself. You have taken an inventory of where you want to be, what steps you are taking to get there, what more you need to do, and who or what can help you get there faster. As you seek to find, build, manage, or strengthen your personal brand, this assessment will help you clearly understand who you are. Before you can build a brand and be known for something, you have to understand what product you are selling and what you want others to know. Refer to this exercise often and keep it in front of you as you discover more about yourself. Use it also as motivation to begin taking the steps to access your hopes and dreams.

The first and primary element in developing your personal brand is having an intimate knowledge of yourself.

Chapter 2K

Know What You Want to Be Known For

In This Chapter

- Leaving a lasting Impression
- What people say about you when you are not in the room
- What people say when they are referring you to others
- What people say when they are introducing you

What Do You Want To Be Known For?

Let's start by answering a few questions. Write your responses on the lines below.

What do you want to be known for?

____

____

____

____

What are you are most known by?

____

____

____

____

To create your personal brand, you must have a clear understanding of what you want to be known for. Many of us do not take the time to focus on what we want to be known for and leave it up to others to assign us our own brand identity. Often, this identity is based on subjective or false premises. Having an awareness of what you want to be known for keeps you focused on assessing whether you are projecting the desired attributes of your personal brand. It also helps guide you to the "ACCESS" you need to begin living the life you want to lead. Just think, if you had to wear a name tag but could not write your name, how would you identify yourself? What words or pictures would you choose to select what you want others to know as your true identity?

It's always interesting to see how people identify themselves outside of their given name, but for many of us this exercise requires a lot of thought and time. The next time you are with your friends ask one of them to tell you something that defines who they are without using their name. It's a great exercise and ice breaker. But, it also will expose how little we know about ourselves.

For many of us, what we want to be known for and what we are actually known by are two very different things. This could be a result of attributes we have established in our value system long before we had an awareness of our desired personal brand. For others, it may be a result of personal or physical traits that are permanent or not easily changed. Whatever the case, when you know what you want to be known for you can think through your strengths and weaknesses and uncover the inconsistent elements between what I call "your being" and "your becoming."

Lasting Impressions

There is a famous saying you may have heard: "you never get a second chance to make a first impression." In theory, I agree with this statement, because personal branding is really about impression management. I would, however, offer a slight twist to say: "the first impression you make is the lasting impression others take." In other words, what people think about you formulates a first impression but what you are known for equates to your lasting impression.

Lasting impressions are powerful because they create perceptions, set expectations, draw conclusions, perpetuate stereotypes, and build reputations that can easily produce a personal brand. Unfortunately, if you don't shape your lasting impressions, your personal brand will be defined for you. Even further it will be crafted without your input. This could set you up to be a false representation of yourself.

There are three outcomes of lasting impressions that are worthy of discussion.

1. What people say about you when you are not in the room
2. What people say when they are referring you to others
3. How people introduce you formally

If you have not thought about these three focus areas, begin to think of examples where your brand has been displayed in each context.

What People Say When You Are Not in the Room

Have you ever thought about what people are saying about you when you are not in a room? Many find this thought to be particularly nerve-racking, especially when we believe others are talking about us. The fact is people talk, and whether you like it or not this is not something that you are going to stop or control. Personal branding, however, will give you a game plan for influencing the discussions that take place about you so that *what is said* is consistent with *what is known*.

Let's do another exercise to help you create the elements of your lasting impression.

I want you to write down three words that best describe the lasting impression you want someone to be left with after an encounter with you. In other words, what do you want people to say about you when you are not in the room?

1. ______________________________

2. ______________________________

3. ______________________________

This is an important exercise because you need to consciously know what you want to leave as your lasting impression with those you encounter. It will also help you differentiate yourself so you can capitalize on personal or professional opportunities that come your way.

You should be able to answer this question in a matter of seconds. Think about it and reflect for a second. The longer it takes for you to know what you want to be known for, the more it suggests you lack supreme knowledge of yourself. And, if you don't know yourself, you can't expect others to:

Know you,
Refer you,
Select you,
Hire you,
Promote you,
And most importantly,
"Get you."

I've learned that people who don't "get you" won't "let you" create another opportunity to be "gotten." This is just another way to say lasting impressions really last. When you are focused on what you want to be known for you can proactively manage the impressions you leave with others.

Now let's go back to what is said about you when you are not in the room. The reason that this is somewhat uncomfortable for most people is that we do not always take the time to understand the rooms where our brand will be on display. Think for a moment, and look at your appointment calendar, meeting schedule, class schedule, or any other schedule that has you slated to be somewhere at a specific time. Those are all confirmed opportunities for your personal brand to be on display. But what about the meeting schedules, class schedules, and appointments that are not on your calendar or you have not been invited to attend? These events are dates, times, and people who will also get an opportunity to interact with your brand. The point I am making is that to effectively manage your personal brand you should be just as aware of the opportunities where you will be talked about, thought about, praised about, or heckled, so that you can be more deliberate in seeking to make an impression based on what you want to be known for.

Here's a quick exercise that you can do at home, school, work, or the office.

A. Pick a day of the week and write out your schedule for the day, listing all the meetings that you will attend or appear in person and the attendees at those meetings.
B. Now select someone in your immediate personal, academic, or professional circle who is close enough to you to know what you do and how you create value. Find out or envision what meetings, appointments, or important conversations are on that person's schedule for the day and the other attendees to those meetings.
C. Look at your meetings and the meetings of the person you selected to see if there is any overlap in attendees. If so, then you will have identified key sources for establishing an impression and a live passenger vehicle to help your brand travel to the room where you will not be present.

I know what you may be saying. This sounds kind of clandestine and for some this may feel a little uncomfortable or contrived.

Personal branding is not something that you have to do behind the scenes. For many it is an uncomfortable thing because it does not always feel comfortable to deliberately focus on ourselves and to actually plan how we are going to promote ourselves and our accomplishments to others. Personal branding, however, is essential to achieving success. The key take away from this concept is awareness and anticipation. If you are not aware of the opportunities to brand yourself, you may not be directed to leave a favorable impression. If you cannot anticipate the opportunities that will present themselves to favorably demonstrate your brand through capability, you may not be prepared when they occur. So as you begin to think about what you want to be known for, begin to be more aware of what you want people to say about you when you are not in the room as an effective way to guide your personal brand and the impression you leave with others.

What People Say When They Are Referring You to Others

Have you ever asked someone for a recommendation or referral? It's always flattering to have the opportunity to refer someone you trust, admire, and want to support. But how often do you go back to those people and ask them to explain why they wrote the referral or recommendation they provided? Asking someone for a referral or recommendation is one of the best ways to find out what people think about you and confirm what you are known for. Think about it. This is a safe environment that is nonthreatening to the receiver of the recommendation and flattering to the giver of the referral.

You can ask for a recommendation for just about anything and more often than not the people you ask will give you a favorable rating. So to establish greater recognition of your personal brand, try a new twist on obtaining a recommendation or referral.

A. Identify something you would like to be recommended for or a referral that you would like to get for an opportunity
B. Select three people who you will ask for a recommendation letter or referral
C. Pick one of those three people and ask them to develop your recommendation letter based *only* from the feedback of a mutual contact you both have in common but has no knowledge of this exercise
D. Ask for all of the recommendation letters back

E. Compare the recommendation letter of the people who gave you a direct recommendation to the content of the recommendation letter that was built from a mutual contact two steps removed from the process

This is an effective way to test if there is consistency between what you think you are known for and what others have to say about you.

How Others Introduce You Formally

Have you ever stopped and listened to how people introduce you to others? Whether it is a long or short introduction, the key words that come out naturally are a telltale indicator of what you are known for. We often don't pay enough attention to the power of an introduction.

Let's stop for a second and think about how great brands are introduced to us as consumers. If you think of the introduction of the latest version of a Nike basketball sneaker, the introduction of a new Sony PlayStation video game, or of a new BMW series automobile, there is great fanfare around the introduction of these products. A deluge of advertising, billboards, in-store promotions, and word of mouth create a buzz that allows you to walk away with a clear understanding of the brand and the product being sold. An effective brand product introduction strategy has six elements. They include:

1. Advertising of the brand (logo, jingle, color identification, slogan)
2. Spotlight on the actual product being sold
3. A reputable source who is recommending the product or shown experiencing the product favorably
4. Details of the functionality or features of the product
5. Information about how to purchase or access more information about the product
6. A unique selling point that differentiates the product and brand from competing product offers

So let's relate this to your personal brand and give you a formula to influence how you are introduced by others. As a general rule, if you want others to have a clear understanding of how to introduce you, you should have a clear understanding of how you want to be introduced. There are six elements, which I call the art of the introduction. Each element has six values associated with it that drive the effectiveness of your personal brand. Let's explore them further.

The Art of the Introduction

1. Who you are: Name value
2. What you call yourself: Title value
3. The scope of the territory in your immediate domain: Context value
4. The highest ranking official that you associate yourself with in the scope of what you do: Association value
5. The general role you play in the operations of your immediate domain: Role and contribution value
6. A unique skill, talent, or recognition that you are known for: Accolade value

Pay Attention

Have you ever studied the way you introduce yourself to others in a personal or professional setting? When you think about it, we have been introducing ourselves since the very first moments when we were able to say our names. But when you think about how much attention we really pay to the way we introduce ourselves, for many of us it is not something we study or consciously focus on. However, the way you introduce yourself or the way you are introduced has a significant impact on how you are perceived and subsequently on your personal brand.

So let's break down each component of the Art of the Introduction so you have a general understanding of how to apply this concept and put it into action.

Name Value

Who you are?

The first and most prominent component of an introduction is your name. Your name and its distinction signifies who you are, conveys a perception of how you view yourself, and may draw reference to your background, nationality, or heritage. Although we do not name ourselves at birth, our names carry a specific value or cachet that advertises our personal brand. Like products, some names are received in our minds like logos. Some names provide an inviting ring like a TV commercial jingle or slogan, and some names give us a strongly negative or positive association. For example, let's think about two names. Write down the first thing that comes to mind when you see the name.

Mr. Redd Hate____________________________________

Ms. Flora Love____________________________________

Let me see if I can read your mind. I'm going to guess that for Mr. Redd Hate you may have drawn an association to rage, burning, or someone not so pleasant. For Ms. Flora Love, you may immediately think of flowers, sunshine, hearts, love, and someone with a positive attitude that you would not mind being around. This is an example of how natural associations and immediate perceptions can be built from your name, especially when you have a name that has a specific meaning beyond your first or last name.

So as it relates to knowing what you want to be known for it is important to know and understand the immediate perceptions and connotations that are built from your name. This level of awareness will help you anticipate natural barriers you may have to overcome in the way you introduce yourself that may otherwise undermine your personal brand value. On the flip side, if you have a name that draws immediate positive energy, you should be aware of the expectations that will be set and the assumptions that will be made about your personal brand well before you get to share the rest of your introduction.

The best way to assure you are aware of your name value is to test this concept. So let's do an exercise:

Write your name here ____________________________________

Call a friend or colleague who you do not know that well and ask him or her to tell you the first thing that comes to mind when they hear your name. Ask for an honest response even if their response is not something that you may want to hear.

Write down his or her response here ____________________________

Try this exercise with as many people as you can to get a fair sample of responses. If you generally get a response that is not consistent with the perception you have of yourself or what you want to be known for, then you know that you may have to address your name connotation as part of how you introduce yourself. This will help to take the attention away from your name and place the emphasis on the other attributes of your personal brand.

Don't Be Tone Deaf

There is one variable when it comes to creating name value in an introduction. It is the tone of your voice or the tone of the voice of the person introducing you. You want to have your name said in a tone that conveys confidence, credibility, and character. If you are introducing yourself, an upright posture and a deep breath before speaking will help you to belt out your name with this type of conviction.

If you will be introduced by someone else, especially if it will be in a formal or professional setting, try to find out the tone of voice of the person introducing you so you can anticipate or influence how your brand will be displayed. Taking this to the most extreme level, you may want to tape yourself saying your name and give it to the person introducing you so they can practice accordingly to represent your brand accurately. You may be asking, is that really necessary? Or you may feel taking it to this extreme measure of taping yourself may result in you being perceived as anal retentive and a whole host of other adjectives. The point I am trying to make is that names matter, and how you say your name will have a direct impact in supporting what you want to be known for.

Title Value

What do you call yourself?

The use of your title in an introduction will most strongly give others a sense of your credibility. What you call yourself—your title—will convey a perception of accomplishment, career distinction, and maturity that will create an immediate impression in the minds of others. I call this title value. There are millions of titles that we use to describe who we are in our personal or professional lives. It's important to make a distinction that a title is not a role. A title is an identifier that you use to communicate what you call yourself, or what you want others to know about your level of accomplishment in the context of your working domain.

Similar to how advertisers spotlight the product in an ad or TV commercial to capture the consumer's attention, your title is the spotlight in your introduction that will capture and draw others into you. State your title right after your name so that people make the connection between your name and your accomplishments. In other words, your brand and product. The media has trained us to make quick associations between a brand and a product. A great example of this correlation is Kleenex (brand) and tissue (product). As this relates to your personal brand, you want your introduction or the way you are introduced to establish a quick association of your name (the brand) and your title (the product).

Context Value

What is the scope of territory in your immediate domain?

Once you have established a strong connection between your name and your title, it is essential to provide others with a sense of your scope of territory. In other words, how far reaching is the impact of your efforts? This will help others place your accomplishments in broader context which further adds credibility to your personal brand. I call this context value. Advertisers like to use celebrity endorsers of their product to show the exact context of the product's appeal. For example, a consumer may say, "If Tiger Woods would use this golf club to hit a ball, it must be a good product." Similarly, if others say you are responsible for national or global initiatives, a superintendent of the largest school district in the county, or lead the planning for the world's largest fair, then you must have significant impact and thus will rate you even higher on the perception scale.

Words like global, national, world's most, largest, oldest, historic, leading, only, and best-rated all convey a sense of scope and impact. When introducing yourself or when being introduced by others, incorporating scope and impact will help drive positive association for your brand.

Association Value

What or who is the highest ranking official or entity that you associate yourself with in the scope of what you do?

Advertisers like to display product features in ads to help people make the connection between brand, product, and benefits. In essence, what they are doing is creating an association that "this brand" of "this product" will yield or get you closer to "this result." When we relate this concept to how we introduce ourselves or how we are introduced, it is effective to make this same connection. Your introduction should convey, for example, "this person" with "this title" is associated with "this benefit." I call this association value. In a corporate or professional setting, one of the ways you can establish this is by mentioning the highest ranking official or entity that you associate yourself with in the scope of what you do. For example, phrases like "I work in conjunction with the president's office," or "I work for John Smith, who serves as secretary general for the Department of State." These are examples of using association value to raise your brand profile in an introduction. Association value helps others understand who you are directly connected to and how a relationship with you may impact results or provide an added benefit to getting wider exposure. It also supports your brand by giving you added credibility in the context of what your title says about you.

Role and Contribution Value

What is the general role you play in the operations of your immediate domain?

A product's features outline the benefits that one will gain from the purchase or usage of the product. A product's benefits are what the product actually delivers. This is most typically known as its performance. At the end of the day, a product's performance is what ultimately drives the greatest long term value for the product and its brand. In other words, if you have a great brand with excellent product features, endorsed by the most reputable sources, and promoted by the most enticing advertising campaign, it will not return, retain, or increase long term value if the performance of the product is not superior. When we liken this concept to how we introduce ourselves, it exposes the importance of describing your role in driving performance as a key element of your introduction.

As I mentioned previously, there is a distinction between one's title and one's role. Your title is an identifier that you use to communicate what you call yourself. In other words, it is what you want others to know about your level of accomplishment in the context of your working domain. Your role is a direct statement of what you do. Putting it simply, from your role someone should be able to clearly understand the actions that you take to create impact.

Often when introducing ourselves, we tend to skip over an explanation of our role and default to our title to explain what we do. An effective introduction, however, will include details of your role. This communicates the performance contribution you make as result of who you are (brand), what you call yourself (product), the scope of your responsibilities (context), and who you work with or for (association). I call this role and contribution value. When executed well, the communication of your role and contribution will augment the perceived value of what others know you by, thus increasing the value of your personal brand.

Accolade Value

What is a unique skill or talent that you are known for that distinguishes you from other people?

The most memorable products have unique features or capabilities that distinguish them from other products in their category. Think about a product with a unique feature. Let's consider the Roomba robot vacuum. A revolutionary product for our time, it has immediate recall among consumers and stands out over regular vacuum models due to its unique design, features, and conceptual performance. The uniqueness of this product creates an even stronger connection between brand and product such that the category of robot vacuums can be synonymous with the Roomba brand, and the Roomba brand is synonymous with robot vacuums.

The advantage of having a strong brand-to-product association driven by uniqueness is that the product and brand become the category which creates exponential opportunities to increase the product's long term value. The challenge of such a strong association is that if the product brand seeks to be known for something different or to be identified with a product line outside its category, it may be difficult to shed the perception of its original attribute.

As you think more about this concept and how it relates to how you introduce yourself, recognize that uniqueness of skill, talent, or a noteworthy accolade can be a major strength in creating value for your personal brand. I call this accolade value. For example, as a saxophone player, I often play my horn at the start or end of a speaking presentation. As I travel around the country, many have identified me for my saxophone playing just as much as they have identified me for my speaking. Playing the saxophone is a part of my personal brand and is an attribute I use to inspire others. "Inspire" is my brand name and as a result there is a great synergy and strength that I draw from the uniqueness of playing the saxophone. When I am introduced by others, I am often tagged at the end of the introduction as being a saxophone player, which supports my personal brand.

So as you think about the way you introduce yourself or how you are introduced by others, think about the unique qualities, skills, talent, or accolades that you possess and use them as a strength to increase the value of the impression you leave with others and a signifying element of your personal brand.

(K)reating Your Introduction

Before we proceed, let's build your personal brand introduction based on the six values. This will give you a formula for introducing yourself and a tool to direct others on how best to introduce you. Start by recording your responses to each value, and then let's put them together to form your personal brand introduction.

Here's an example.

Kaplan Mobray is a best-selling author, acclaimed motivational speaker, life coach, and expert on the topic of personal branding. He is globally recognized as a leading authority on personal branding and is a popular speaker and teacher of life and career inspiration techniques. He is a frequent contributor to *The Wall Street Journal*, the *Harvard Business Review*, *BusinessWeek* , and other nationally-recognized magazines and journals. He has inspired millions nationally and internationally with his message of building your personal brand. In addition to *The 10Ks of Personal Branding*, he is the author of four other books and the founder of 10K Branding, LLC, a provider of career and life improvement workshops. In his spare time, Kaplan can be found headlining in jazz clubs as a professional saxophone player. He lives in New York.

Let's dissect this introduction to examine how I positioned each of my values.

Name Value

- Who you are
  Write your first and last name: **Kaplan Mobray**

Title Value

- What you call yourself
  Write your official title or what you call yourself**: is a best-selling author, acclaimed motivational speaker, life coach, and expert on the topic of personal branding.**

Context Value

- The scope of territory in your immediate domain
  Write the scope of your domain: **He is globally recognized as a leading authority on personal branding and is a popular speaker and teacher of life and career inspiration techniques.**

Association Value

- The highest ranking official or entity that you associate yourself with in the scope of what you do
  List the name of the highest ranking official that you associate yourself with in the scope of what you do: **He is a frequent contributor to *The Wall Street Journal*, the *Harvard Business Review*, *BusinessWeek*, and other nationally-recognized magazines and journals.**

Role and Contribution Value

- The general role you play in the operations of your immediate domain

Write down the role you play in the operations of your working domain: **He has inspired millions nationally and internationally with his message of building your personal brand.**

Accolade Value

- A unique skill, talent, or recognition that you are known for that distinguishes you among others
  List a unique skill, talent, or recognition that you are known for or that distinguishes you among others: **In addition to *The 10Ks of Personal Branding*, he is the author of four other books and the founder of 10K Branding, LLC a provider of career and life improvement workshops. In his spare time, Kaplan can be found headlining in jazz clubs as a professional saxophone player. He lives in New York.**

Now it's your turn. Let's (k)reate your personal brand introduction using the six values we learned above.

Your Personal Brand Introduction

Name Value

- Who you are
  Write your first and last name: ________________ ________________

Title Value

- What you call yourself
  Write your official title or what you call yourself: ________________

Context Value

- The scope of territory in your immediate domain
  Write the scope of your domain: ______________________________

Association Value

- The highest ranking official that you associate yourself with in the scope of what you do
  List the name of the highest ranking official that you associate yourself with in the scope of what you do: ______________________________
  ____

Role and Contribution Value

- The general role you play in the operations of your immediate domain

Write down the role you play in the operations of your working domain: ______________________________

Accolade Value

- A unique skill, talent, or recognition that you are known for that distinguishes you among others
  List a unique skill, talent, or recognition that you are known for that distinguishes you among others: ______________________
  ____

Now write your statement in paragraph form to craft your complete introduction.

____

____

____

____

If you have completed the lines above, you have successfully mastered the 10K Branding Art of the Introduction. Great job! Use this framework to help guide you to a powerful introduction of yourself. As you do, you will create greater value for your personal brand and truly allow what you want to be known for to be consistent with how you present yourself.

What You Notice Versus What You Remember

Take out a piece of chocolate or your preferred treat and begin to eat it. (Crunch-crunch-crunch-crunch-crunch-crunch-crunch-crunch-crunch-crunch-crunch-crunch-crunch-crunch.) Did you know the average person takes thirty chews to eat a piece of candy?[3]

This may seem like a useless fact, but try to notice how many times you chew or crunch the next time you eat a piece of candy. Here's my point. Most people don't notice how many times they chew, but they can recall what they ate. Similarly, you may not notice what lasting impressions you leave with someone, but I can bet you remember the meeting place or encounter.

When you focus on your personal brand, you gain a heightened awareness of what you want to be known for and you begin to notice more details about yourself. You will notice details like your posture, tone of voice, response time in answering requests, who you help, and who you refer to others. All of these elements, normally considered small details, are attributes that when managed well can better position you for opportunity and leave a favorable impression.

As we close this chapter, use these thoughts on lasting impressions to help gain an understanding of what you want to be known for. Lasting impressions are the most important impressions to manage. The way you introduce yourself will say a lot about the perception of your value. And, knowing what you want to be known for is an important step in accomplishing the outcomes you desire and the personal brand you wish to convey.

The longer it takes for you to know what you want to be known for, the more it suggests you lack supreme knowledge of yourself.

Chapter 3K

Know How to Be Consistent

In This Chapter

- The importance of being consistent
- Correlation between your passion and personal brand
- The psychology of consistency

The secret of success is consistency of purpose.

-Benjamin Disraeli

Having a Consistent Brand

If you have ever traveled outside your home country you notice and appreciate the familiarity of major brands. From golden arches to a red and white can of soda to a coffee lounge with green awnings, great brands provide familiarity in a world full of uncertainty. The process of global branding is really a process of building worldwide trust. Great product brands are able to sustain consumer appeal in foreign markets because they establish a universal expectation of trust that keeps consumers loyal, happy, and safe. It is a continual process and marketers must monitor world conditions daily to ensure that the uncertainty or volatility of a foreign country or government system does not impact the trust and appeal that consumers associate with their product brand.

Building your personal brand is also a continual process. It is an extension of how you speak, think, your writing style, personal appearance, track record for performance, your outlook on life, and many other characteristics. You want to create a seamless string of perceptions that associate you with the brand you want to build regardless of the situation or context in which your brand is displayed.

When you think of the most recognized brands today, one of the first things that comes to mind is "consistency." The most regarded brands all deliver a consistent expectation of quality and other product attributes that somehow keep you loyal to their product. But what about your product attributes? What is it that you consistently deliver that keeps others loyal to you?

Write your response to the question below.

What is it that you consistently deliver that keeps others loyal to you?

____

This is a tough question. You may know why you buy the same brands of your favorite products, but do you really know why people continually come back to you, select you for opportunities, or give you more responsibility?

It's all based on trust. Your personal brand sets a precedence and expectation for what you will deliver. So, your ability to be consistent will help you achieve a level of differentiation that allows your strengths to resonate and your brand to shine.

Most of us do not sit and analyze why others choose us for things. In fact, it is not something you may even know how to find out. You may think it just happens naturally or it is because you are liked or have a solid reputation. The reality is, people are loyal to people they trust, admire, respect, or want to help. Similarly, consumers buy products they trust, admire, respect, or want to support. The more knowledge you have of why people are loyal to you, the more aware you will be of the importance of having consistency in your personal brand attributes. Let's explore further how to find out why people are loyal to you.

Why Are People Loyal to Your Brand?

It is not always the most comfortable thing to ask a friend or colleague why they are loyal to you. In fact, it is quite awkward. There are three ways however to find out why people are loyal to you and thus why they support your brand.

1. Ask for advice
2. Ask for a donation
3. Invite someone to attend an event

Asking for Advice

When you ask someone for advice and counsel, it usually takes three to five seconds for that person to make a decision to fully support you, support you with reservation, or reject the notion of giving you advice and support. This is in fact the same amount of time that people generally take to make a first impression. Dr. Marianne LaFrance, a professor at Yale University and director of the study First Impressions and Hair Impressions, says that "One has only three seconds to make a good first impression." So if it takes the same amount of time to make a first impression as it does to make a decision to support someone, we can infer that people make decisions to support someone based on the same cognitive filter they use to create a first impression.

When you ask for advice the verbal and nonverbal response you get from someone in the first three seconds will indicate their level of support for you, which may also reveal how they perceive your personal brand. Quick responses to help and offer advice, accompanied by forward movement and direct eye contact, reveal a positive response to your personal brand. Delayed reaction, accompanied by a pensive movement backwards, and less direct eye contact indicate a slight reservation in one's willingness to offer help and may reveal a negative or neutral perception of your personal brand.

Asking For a Donation

Have you ever asked someone for a donation to support you for a charitable activity? Perhaps you have been involved in a bowl-a-thon, walk-a-thon, or something else-a-thon. If you have, then you know how difficult the task of raising funds and garnering support can be.

For most people, the decision making process to donate money to a charitable activity begins with them thinking about the person asking for the donation. You can very easily evaluate the strength of your personal brand by assessing people's response to you when raising money for charity. The fact is, if people do not support your personal brand, they most often will not pledge their support for the cause you represent. Conversely, if they value and favorably perceive your personal brand, it is more likely that they will also give a donation for the charity to which you have pledged your support.

Inviting Someone to Attend an Event

Have you ever invited someone to attend an event and they decline? You invite them a second time and they decline. You invite them a third time and they decline. At some point, after making excuses for the person, you get the hint that they really do not want to attend the event. Have you ever internalized this result and asked yourself if they declined because of you? This is a common scenario and I am sure at some point in your life you have experienced or know someone who has faced this situation.

When you invite someone to attend an event, attend with you, or attend for you, in essence you are asking that person to be a representative of your personal brand. I acknowledge that not every declined invitation can be attributed to the person extending the invite, but a recurring pattern of excuses and declines typically signify a lack of perceived value in the brand of the person doing the inviting. In other words, people do not attend events with and for people they do not support.

In short, each of the above concepts involves some form of asking for something as a means to receive feedback. The point I am trying to emphasize is that there are ways to test your brand value with others. It's an important thing to do as you seek to manage your brand with consistency. When you know why people accept or reject you, you are in a better position to manage your personal brand effectively. Having a focus on what you deliver that keeps others loyal to you will give you an awareness of the personal brand attributes that you can consistently use to create opportunity.

Your Passion and Personal Brand

We often overlook the importance of having consistency in our personal brand because we may not identify the connection between our personal passions and our brand. For example, we may believe who we are outside of work, or who we are when we are doing our favorite activity, is someone and something totally different than who we are in our professional occupation, job, or career.

Personal branding is about living your life to a code of consistent attributes that transcend work and play. There is a direct correlation between your personal passions and your personal brand. Those who are able to find it end up living a more complete life and may reach greater levels of success. Let's explore this further. Please complete your responses to the questions below.

Exercise:

Write down three to five of your personal passions or hobbies to which you devote a significant amount of your time.

____

____

____

____

Now write down the attributes you live or experience through these personal passions. For example, if one of my personal passions was fishing, one of the attributes that I live through this activity is patience. What would you say to someone who wants to be a fisherman but has no patience? I bet you could think of a couple of suggestions.

Write the attributes you experience or lessons you learn through your personal passions or hobbies.

____

____

____

____

Write down the three words that describe the lasting impression you want to leave with others after an encounter with you.

____________, ____________, ____________,

Write down your job, occupation, or career aspirations.

____

____

____

____

Take a look back at your responses. Is there a correlation between the hobbies and activities that you are most passionate about and your personal brand? How do the attributes or lessons that you experience from these activities relate to the three words that describe the lasting impression you leave on others? Do they all demonstrate your personal brand? This exercise is designed to make you think about the connection between *what you are interested in* and *who you are.*

Perceiving Our Free Time

For many of us, it is not apparent that others may perceive us by what we do outside of work or school as our "real self." In actuality, we are our truest self in the moments when we control how we use our time. In other words, what we do when we personally direct our time is a true expression of the self we live in the personal direction of our brand. Keep this thought in mind as you analyze the elements of your personal brand that are derived from your personal passions and your life aspirations. You will be inspired as you begin to the make the connection between the two elements of your life. This view will also help you begin formulating consistent elements of your brand that you can demonstrate in a variety of settings. In essence, you are building a global personal brand.

Finding Your Consistency

The consistency between your personal and professional life activities may not be so apparent. You may have unrelated responses across each category for the questions you answered above. I encourage you to begin to find the links between what you are most passionate about and your life and career aspirations. Ultimately, there should be a deep connection between the two. When you begin to link them, you will begin to build consistency in your personal brand and realize greater fulfillment in your life.

Here's an example of a consistent brand and personal passion based on the exercise you just completed.

Name	Jane Smith
Hobbies	Playing billiards, archery, and drawing
Lessons learned from hobbies	Precision, focus, and concentration
Lasting impressions I wish to leave with others	I am detail oriented, organized, and punctual
Occupation	Civil engineer

When you take a look at this example above, you see that the elements of Jane Smith's personal hobbies and interests (archery, billiards, drawing) have a direct correlation to the skills needed for her occupation (civil engineer). Civil engineers need to be precise, must be able to focus sharply on details, and should be adept at drawing up plans for the various projects and assessments of roads and bridge structures that they are responsible for overseeing. Jane has a solid outline of personal and professional consistency.

If you have very unrelated responses across each of the lines in this exercise I am not suggesting that you go out and change your job or lifestyle. I am advocating, however, that you seek to find the connection between the two.

The Professor of Dance

In building your personal brand, what you are striving for is consistency in your brand and the personal and professional interests that you use to define yourself. For example, there is a woman I know who is a physics professor by day and ballroom dancer at night. Each day these two occupations take her to two seemingly different worlds; the world of academia and the world of performing arts. She finds comfort knowing that her escape from a draining day in the classroom is to let her soul free through dance. Over the past year she began to wonder if her passion for dance was taking a toll on her enthusiasm to teach.

For some reason she was not getting through to her students. They would no longer volunteer to take part in class exercises, would not ask questions on the course material, and were becoming delinquent in turning in homework assignments. She herself could not wait to get out of the classroom as soon as the bell sounded to run to the dance studio. Further, she realized that she was beginning to avoid the students who wanted to stay after class for remedial help with assignments.

Paralyzed with fear that she was not succeeding in her profession and would soon receive complaints from students and their parents, she made a decision to try to find more consistency in her personal and professional brand. One day, when preparing for a lesson plan on the laws of motion, she decided to create a new formula to help the students understand the technical definition of force. Instead of force = mass x acceleration, she introduced a new concept. She wrote on the board: dance = acceleration x movement, and proceeded to do a waltz all around the classroom. The students looked perplexed and started to chuckle. At first she did not know if they were laughing with her or at her but she continued to waltz all around the classroom chanting "Dance equals acceleration times movement."

After a couple of minutes, she stopped and froze right in the center of the room. The students looked in amazement and wondered what to say. The professor had extended her leg up and around her neck and was now balancing on one foot. If you saw her you would say she was imitating a flamingo, but in dance language she was doing a rather difficult full leg extension. She said to the class, "Now that I have your complete attention, please open your book to page 137. We will be discussing the elements of the laws of motion." Every student opened their book and that day she had no problems getting her students to participate in volunteer assignments.

This exercise went on to become a daily routine and branded her on campus as the professor of dance. She went on to begin every class in this manner and found a way to demonstrate true consistency in her personal and professional life activities. As a result, she became a better educator and found a new way to teach complex physics concepts in a manner that would engage her students.

The Psychology of Consistency

As human beings, we are taught to recognize patterns and sequences that we define and put into categories. These categories help us better understand the pattern or sequence in a way that creates meaning. For example: ABCD ... 1234 ... red, yellow, green. Similarly, personal branding is about creating recognizable patterns and sequences that allow you to define yourself to others in a way that helps others better understand your value. My goal in this chapter is to get you to become more conscious of the patterns and sequence of activities in your personal and professional life so you can define your value and not have it defined for you.

To increase your awareness of your personal brand consistency, you must start with an awareness of what your consistent actions say about you and how you internalize your brand each day. Reflect for a moment on what you do when you wake up in the morning. Are there specific things that you do consistently? And what is your mind-set as you begin each day? What are the consistent thoughts that you internalize as a part of your personal brand?

It has been demonstrated that the way you start your day shapes how you feel and the outcomes you experience. Martin Seligman, a former head of the American Psychological Association, conducted a study in 2002 on positive psychology. In his research he found that people with high positive psychological capital experience better life outcomes, including performing better on their jobs. The research further supports the notion that positive psychology leads to greater satisfaction and stable personal and professional growth.[4]

Stable personal and professional growth is an outcome of achieving consistency in your personal brand. You can conclude that your actions in the context of your environment and your mind-set in the context of how you approach each day will shape the perception that others have of you. So to build your personal brand, focus on the consistent actions and behaviors that define who you are and the mind-set that you carry as part of your daily routines. Together they will shape greater value for your personal brand and help you to realize greater fulfillment in your life.

Your ability to be consistent will help you achieve a level of differentiation that allows your strengths to resonate.

Chapter 4K

Know How to Accept Failure as Part of Building Your Personal Brand

In This Chapter

- Learning from failure
- The benefits of taking risks

Seek Failure

Have you ever thought about what failure means to you? Is it something that you run from, try to avoid, or is it something that you embrace? Think about the last time you failed. Did you fail because whatever you were doing was part of a larger goal and you had to experience this failure in order to keep going? Or did you fail because you had no plan? Often we fail because we have no plan. So here's a concept I'd like to you think about. **Seek failure.** That's right. Seek failure. I bet no one has ever encouraged you to seek failure before. Let me explain.

The Merriam-Webster dictionary defines failure as "a failing to perform a duty or expected action." Sometimes we don't meet objectives because we took a risk. When we take a risk, we extend ourselves outside the zone of what we define as "achievable." This journey, and the process of living it, brings us closer to an understanding of the outer limits of what I call our "capacity for capability." These are the things we are capable of achieving if we reduced the barriers of fear that hold us back. By extending yourself outside your comfort zone, you allow yourself to experience greater depth and create a broader definition of what is possible. You don't know what you're capable of until you push yourself to new limits, so seek failure. Here's another thought to reflect on. Have you ever had a transforming setback in your life or career?

Write a description of that setback on the lines below.

____

____

Think about that setback. Now think about who and what you have become as a result of it. Now think about your personal brand and your life activities, and the impression you leave with others. How has that event contributed to the brand you live today? Learning to accept failure and to learn from failure in the context of a larger goal is vital to the process of discovering your brand. Let's explore this further.

Think back to a time when you took a risk. What did it feel like?

____

____

What are three words that you would use to describe the outcome of that risk?

1. ________________

2. ________________

3. ________________

Now write the three words that best describe the lasting impression you want someone to be left with after an encounter with you.

1. ________________

2. ________________

3. ________________

How do the outcomes of your risk taking measure up with the impression you leave with others?

For many of us, there is little correlation between outcomes from risk taking and our wish list for impression-making. This assumes we experience taking risks as something negative. For others, you may find that your risk taking has led to reward-making, and there is a direct link to the impression you leave with others. I have my own personal definition of failure that I use often when faced with difficult challenges or unsuccessful outcomes. I like to think of failure as "a reward to those who accept its challenge and the nutrients of its journey." The nutrients of the journey are what build the foundation for the character behind your personal brand. Have you ever heard someone say, "That person has character"? What do they mean by this? What do you interpret that to mean?

Building Character

Is character a product of one's value system? Or is it your interpretation of how someone managed through a challenge? Character is built not birthed. It is often bestowed upon one who has achieved, experienced, triumphed, and overcome. When you fail, you allow yourself the opportunity to overcome, which builds character. Your character is the skeleton that holds your personal brand in place. So as you begin to think about your brand, begin to include an acceptance of failure and the things that may not have gone so right in your life. At the end of the day we are just as much the product of our failures as we are our successes.

How Failure Changed My Life

Over the course of my life I have failed over twenty thousand times and have learned over twenty thousand lessons in the process. The biggest lesson, however, came when I was six years old. I was learning to play the drums at the time, and had been practicing for my first music recital. Like most kids at age six, life seemed so easy, so carefree. My biggest concerns were what sugar cereal I would eat for breakfast and what toy I would play with after dinner. In between eating and playing I was learning to bang on the drums. Perhaps my parents put me in drum lessons to help me channel all my energy so they could get some sleep at night, or maybe it was so I could play in the church band. Whatever the original intent, this experience changed my life and to them I am forever grateful. I practiced for the recital for weeks. Every day for four hours I played rhythms from the tap-tap book for beginner drummers.

For a six year old, I had a good handle on keeping the beat and loved to hit the snare drum. My fellow students would stop by and watch me practice to pick up some beats and replicate my technique. The town made a big deal about the upcoming recital and advertised the event on television, the radio, and on posters. I think I even saw my name on one of the posters. It was to be the recital of all recitals. All the best kid musicians in the neighborhood would be there to show their stuff. At age six, this was the biggest event to hit my life. I was finally going to play on a stage.

After weeks of practice and visualizing my performance, recital night was finally here. There were about two hundred and fifty people in the audience, but to me it might as well have been a ten-thousand-person auditorium. I saw all my friends and their parents who came out to see me play. I was ready to show the world what I was made of.

After nearly forty minutes of performances I finally heard my name. The announcer shouted, "Kaplan Mobray, come to the stage. Kaplan will play drums to the song 'Old MacDonald Had a Farm.'" The crowd cheered as I walked up to the drums and picked up my sticks. I looked over to my parents and gave them my signature slanted smile. I just knew they were going to be proud of what I was about to do. The piano player started the accompaniment and gave me the nod that it was okay to join in. I picked up my sticks and then it all started. Somehow my hands froze. All of a sudden my hands felt like they were cemented together. No movement, no tapping, no drums. The crowd, now seeming concerned, started to clap for me to help me get going, but I remained stunned and frozen. At this point I also started to wet my pants.

Going up on stage I did not realize how nervous I was, in fact, I had practiced and dreamed about the performance so many times in my head I felt like I had already given a great show. After about three minutes of silence and an obvious breakdown on my part, my dad rose from the audience and came up to rescue me from the stage. I almost could not look at him because we made a deal that I would give a great performance. He said, "What happened up there? I know you can do it!" The crowd, now trying to get back to the show, turned their attention to the announcer who announced the next act.

Another forty minutes went by and the recital was finally over. My friends and family looked over at me and did not know whether to congratulate me for going up on stage or run away from me for embarrassing them. I felt both. My dad, seeing that I was about to cry, quickly grabbed my hand and pulled me back to the stage. He tracked down the piano player and asked if he could come back on stage and play Old MacDonald one more time. Shaking, I picked up my sticks and began to play. Tap-Tap-Tap-Tap, Tap-Tap-Tap, Tap-Tap-Tap-Tap-Tap. I then looked over at my dad and shouted "I played it!"

He looked back at me and said, "Yes, you did son! Well done."

There were still some onlookers from the recital who saw what happened and all of a sudden I heard a thunderous roar of applause. I turned around and saw my family and friends smiling. I had redeemed myself and could leave the recital knowing that I successfully played the song I practiced so tirelessly.

Today, this experience still ranks as one of the biggest lessons I have learned about the importance of failure. Looking back, what I learned was that while I was prepared to succeed through all my hours of practice and rehearsals, I did not prepare myself to fail. In fact, it never entered into my thought process. To this day, in everything I do, I always prepare myself to fail. I have a saying that I use quite often, "If you are not afraid to fail you have all the confidence to succeed." I live by this and it has become an integral part of my personal brand.

So ask yourself, how do you deal with failure? Are there events and experiences that have taught you to seek failure, and if so, how have they contributed to who you are today? Failure is a key component of success and an important element of our personal brand. As you think about who you are, what you want to be known for, and the actions and behaviors that consistently guide your values, think about the role that failure plays as a part of your personal brand. The lessons we learn from failure make us a better brand and they will make you a better you.

Learning from failure is one of the best ways to build for success.

Chapter 5K

Know How to Communicate Your Personal Brand Attributes

In This Chapter

- Communicating your personal brand
- Elevator speech
- Personal brand ambassadors

Communicating Your Personal Brand

This chapter is one of the most important "Ks" in the 10Ks of Personal Branding. The way you communicate your personal brand has a direct effect on the perception others create in their minds about you and your value. When you think about great advertising slogans, the ones that grab your attention, inspire you to act, create fear, make you laugh, or just make you remember back to a time or place that brought you joy, those are the commercials that may in fact influence you to buy the product being sold.

The way you communicate your personal brand attributes will have the same effect. People will buy into you based on how you present yourself and communicate who you are verbally and nonverbally.

Here's a question for you. If you were in an elevator with your company's president, your supervisor, a prospective employer, or someone you really want to impress, what would this person be able to say about you right after he or she got out of the elevator?

____

____

In Chapter 2K I asked you to record the three words that you want to leave as your lasting impression with others you encounter. What were the three words you listed? Write them below.

1. ____________________

2. ____________________

3. ____________________

Let's look at what you wrote. Did the person you wanted to impress have these same three impressions of you based on your response above?

Often we are not aware of the impressions we leave with others because we have not confirmed for ourselves the set of impressions we want to leave as our personal brand.

Saying it With Adjectives

In building my own personal brand, I try to have a set of adjectives that I want someone to use or say about me when I see them. For example, people may comment on my personal appearance, my creativity, and may notice that I am approachable and make an effort to say hello to those I come in contact with. I have a preset understanding that I want people to notice these things about me, so I am more focused in making sure I do my part to allow these results to happen. So I have a particular style in my personal appearance and demeanor, and I let others know right away the crazy ideas I have about business.

As a creative marketer I love to name things. People who know me know that I will not hesitate to create a new name for something or propose a new idea for packaging information so that people will either remember the concept or react to the naming convention. I am also known for being approachable and seeking to help others even in times of utmost inconvenience. These are strong elements of my personal brand, but they are elements that I have incorporated through a deliberate decision to leave this as my lasting impression with others.

So as it relates to jumping in an elevator, when I am in an elevator or confined space with others I smile and try to have something positive to say about the day. I am consistent in my personal appearance and style of dress. It is sometimes noticeable, and I may get a comment about my tie. I am also conscious of ways to creatively give someone a response they may not expect. For example, someone asked me in an elevator about my weekend. I replied, "It was only forty-eight hours, 172,800 seconds out of my week, but I enjoyed every minute of it." My response was seen as creative and I got a chuckle from others on the elevator. This example is an illustration of how you can communicate your personal brand in a variety of methods. What you should take note of is the fact that when you know the lasting impressions you want to leave with others, it actually is much easier to communicate who you are. When people see that you are comfortable in your own skin, confident in who you are, and able to communicate and present yourself in a manner that is consistently distinct, they will be drawn to you. This creates greater value for your personal brand and augments the impressions you leave with others.

The Elevator Speech

Let's explore the concept of the elevator speech. You may have heard the term "elevator speech" before, but do you know what it means and how you can apply it as a part of your personal brand? People often associate the elevator speech as the scenario of what you say when you are in the elevator with your CEO or someone high up in an organization. Over the years, there has been much talk about the importance of having an elevator speech. In fact, in February of 2008, the CNBC television show *The Big Idea*, hosted by advertising mogul Donny Deutsch, devoted a feature of their show to the elevator pitch. The segment was titled "The Elevator Pitch," and contestants had to ride an elevator with a prospective buyer and share their ninety-second business pitch in the hopes of gaining a client.

The elevator speech is essentially a quick, sharp statement of your value that you use when introducing yourself, or in a setting where you want to create an opportunity to be remembered. Unless you are going from the penthouse of a 100-story building to the basement, most elevator rides are approximately thirty seconds long.[5] When you think about it, thirty seconds is also the amount of time an average television commercial lasts.

Commercial Break

In Chapter 1K, I asked you to think about if you had to do a thirty-second commercial on yourself. What would you say? What would be your hook, your jingle, and your slogan?

If you were to analyze the key components of a thirty-second TV commercial, you would understand that an ad is a unit of persuasion with a specific audience in mind, designed to get attention in the cluttered marketplace, and to get a response (immediate or delayed, directly or indirectly).

Persuasion Analysis, a media company, notes that there are five patterns of persuasion that are embedded into a thirty-second TV commercial. They include:

1. Hi (attention-getting)
2. Trust me (confidence-building)
3. You need (desire-stimulating)
4. Hurry (urgency-stressing)
5. Buy (response-seeking)

This sequence focuses your attention on the hidden superstructure (the brand), or the deep structure (the product), common to all ads.[6]

If you relate this to your own personal brand elevator speech, you can see that the goal of an elevator speech is to: persuade an intended audience by getting their attention so they remember you and you position yourself for an opportunity either directly in that encounter or indirectly for the future.

All the World is an Elevator

It's important to know that the elevator speech is not something that only happens in a physical elevator. It may be the two-minute conversation that happens at the mirror in the restroom, or the ten-second conversation that happens while you are waiting in line for lunch. Opportunities for you to create a good impression are lurking around every corner. My goal through this book is to help you get ready for these situations as well as the many other career and life enhancing encounters that you will face over time.

Your elevator speech should be quick and easy to communicate. I consistently use a formula that helps me deliver my elevator speech with impact and effectiveness. Using the principles we have already explored and the five patterns of persuasion, I break my elevator speech down into distinct units. Let's explore them further as you begin to think about positioning your elevator speech.

(K)aplan's Elevator Speech

Awareness	I notice who is in the room, elevator, or confined space, and establish eye contact right away.
Attention-getting	I say hi or smile to get their attention and introduce myself. This lets them know who I am and gives me permission to share more in the interaction.
Confidence-capability	I share a quick tidbit or data point that highlights something me or my team have done successfully.

Desire-stimulating	I indicate how our successes are helping the company or creating impact.
Urgency-stressing	I ask for the opportunity to share more at a later date.
Response-seeking	I bring the conversation to a close and set up a next time to build on our short interaction.

For me this is a quick and natural formula for using time wisely. Although the average elevator ride is thirty seconds, there are many elevator interactions that take place in a matter of ten seconds or less. My goal for the elevator interaction is for the intended audience to walk away having a recall of three things.

1. **Memory of who I am**
   - They should know my name.
2. **Perception of what I am capable of delivering**
   - They should remember an example of when I, or something I was associated with, was successful.
3. **Belief that I can help others**
   - They should leave with a thought about hearing more on how my success or the success of something I was involved with can help benefit others.

I Got That Job!

The funny thing about the elevator speech scenario is that it really happens. Here's a personal example of something that happened to me during an early part of my career. I got a job based on an elevator ride down from the 50th floor to the 44th floor. The whole encounter took approximately six seconds, but to this day they were among the most valuable six seconds I have ever lived in my life.

At the time, I was working for a large banking institution, Citibank North America, as a marketing manager for the New York region. My goal was to one day work in the national marketing group, but at that time the national group was in Chicago and I did not want to relocate from New York.

As it turned out the national marketing director for the company was in town for meetings. I had heard through the rumor mill that he was moving to New York and was looking to establish a national communications group in the next few months, and eventually move the entire national marketing operations to New York. So on the day of his visit, I got up from my cubicle, picked up a sheet of paper from my desk, and got on the elevator to the 50th floor.

The 50th floor was reserved for all of the senior executive offices. It was where the CEO, CFO, COO, and CIO were located. Security was pretty strict, and unless you had a meeting or business there, it was not a place for what I call "non-officials." But that did not stop me from heading to the floor.

I got off the elevator and walked around the floor with that sheet of paper in my hand looking for the national marketing director. If you saw me, you would have thought that I had a confirmed appointment or reason for being on the floor. But the truth was I had no real purpose being up there. My only intention was to put myself in the way of one of the senior executives who was coming out of a meeting so I could be noticed and introduce myself. I was really hoping to bump into the national marketing director who I had heard was up on the 50th floor for the day. I walked the entire floor twice, and to my dismay no one came out of their office. Not even the administrative assistant to one of the executives. It seemed, at that instance, that there was a memo sent to all occupants of the 50th floor alerting them that I was coming and they should all abandon their space. So I regrettably walked back to the elevator lobby to head downstairs.

Well, as it would happen, just as I was getting back on the elevator, who do you think walked in? It was the national marketing director, just the person I was hoping to see. I quickly said hello, trying to hide my amazement that he was in the elevator and that I had just been walking the floor deliberately trying to get his attention. I mentioned in that elevator ride all the great initiatives I had worked on in New York and the successful results our team had achieved, and how I thought they could benefit our offices nationally. I said, "If the successes we have achieved in New York could benefit our offices nationally, I would love to talk with you further."

As I mentioned that interaction took about six seconds. Two weeks later, I got a call from the national marketing director. He said, "Kaplan, as you may know we are moving our national communications operations to New York. I am looking for a national advertising manager, someone who can lead our efforts to manage our advertising initiatives on the national team, and I would love to talk to you about this opportunity." That six-second conversation in the elevator led to a job as national advertising manager for Citibank North America.

As I said, those six seconds were among the most valuable six seconds I have ever lived, because they helped me create an opportunity. They also helped me to realize the importance of being able to communicate my personal brand attributes. I tell you this story to illustrate that the elevator speech really happens! I encourage you to focus on being prepared to quickly communicate your brand value. Even in six seconds. You now have the tools to create your own elevator speech, so begin to give it some focus as you continue to build your personal brand.

I'm So Busy

Have you ever got in an elevator and someone asks you, "How are you doing? How is work going?" and you reply, "I'm so busy!"

The typical reply to your response is "Yeah, me too." In reality, whether you are working in a corporate office building, sitting in a classroom enrolled in a full course load, at home taking care of kids, or working several jobs to make ends meet, we all have busy lives in one form or another. To say "I'm so busy" is becoming as trite as saying "Hello." So in your elevator speech, I want to challenge you to take the opportunity to demonstrate capability. For example, the next time someone in an elevator asks how you are, reply, "I am making some good things happen," or "We are making a difference one day at a time." What you will find is that you immediately begin to brand yourself as someone focused on producing positive outcomes. You will be surprised at how far a simple message in the elevator can travel and how it can lead to great opportunities.

What's that Buzzing Sound?

In advertising, one of the most valuable assets for a company's brand is word-of-mouth advertising.

In the 2007 *Journal of Consumer Research* article titled, "Influentials, Networks and Public Opinion," authors Duncan J. Watts and Peter Sheridan Dodds noted that a central idea in marketing research is that influentials—a minority of individuals who influence an exceptional number of their peers—are important in forming public opinion. This is the essence of word-of-mouth marketing. Word-of-mouth marketing can be described as the spread of information by verbal means, especially recommendations and general information, in an informal, person-to-person manner.

Over the years, word-of-mouth marketing and advertising has actually become a booming industry. Today, associations like the Word of Mouth Marketing Association (WOMMA) are helping companies create consumer-generated media buzz about their brands. Word-of-mouth marketing and advertising has a powerful effect on a company's brand. The Canadian Management Institute estimated that word-of-mouth advertising is one hundred times more powerful and less expensive than traditional advertising.[7]

The way I like to think about it is word-of-mouth creates buzz, and buzz creates sales. As it relates to your personal brand, word-of-mouth advertising, or communicating your brand through others, is an effective way to increase your personal brand value. Just as it is important for a company to know what people are saying about its products, or a producer to know what people are saying about a new movie release, it is essential to know what people are saying about your personal brand. The people who most frequently create buzz are your biggest fans.

Let's start with a question. Write your answers on the lines below.

Do you know your biggest fans? In other words, who are the people in your life, at your job, or at your school who are your loudest cheerleaders? Let's write them down so you can remember these personal or professional contacts later.

Fan #1____

Fan #2____

Fan #3____

Sometimes your biggest fans become what I call your brand ambassadors. If you have a good idea, thought, or perspective that you have shared with them, they (sometimes without your knowing), take it and help spread the word among others about the positives of "you." When this happens your brand begins to travel, and before long people are talking about you, planning for you, considering you for job opportunities, and spreading the good word of your personal brand. This is how opportunities are created. So the next time you hear someone say "Your ears must have been ringing," tell them, "No, my brand was traveling."

You want to have and create as many ambassadors of your brand as possible. It's a great way to maneuver through an organization and a way to get known among leaders. For students, it's a good way to create a positive reputation among multiple contacts within a prospective employer. The more contacts who all share the same opinion of you, the more likely you will land that job.

So how do you create ambassadors for your brand? First ask yourself:

1. Where do you want to go within an organization?
2. Who do you want to influence or be recognized by?
3. Who are the people who can get you closer to the leaders or personal/professional contacts you want to reach?
4. What are the topics of key interest that are "hot buttons" for the people you want to impress?

Exercise:

Write your responses to these questions below:

- In what area would you like to work within your organization?

  ____

- Who do you need to influence or be recognized by?

  ____

- Who are your brand ambassadors? These are the people who can get you closer to the leaders or contacts you are looking to reach or influence.

  ____

  ____

- What are the key themes or topics of interest that are "hot buttons" for those leaders or contacts you wish to impress?

  ____

  ____

- How often do you contact or share information with your ambassadors?

  At least once a week______
  At least once a month_____
  At least once a year_______
  I do not contact my ambassadors______

You want to have and create as many ambassadors of your brand as possible, so you are constantly communicating your personal brand directly or indirectly. Start thinking today about how you communicate your personal brand attributes. Do you have a ready-made statement of your value? Are you developing brand ambassadors? Are you effectively communicating your brand through others? Are you ready for that defining moment when opportunity and preparation meet head-to-head? What can you say about yourself in six seconds that can immediately change your life outcome?

Having a focus on how you communicate your personal brand attributes is one of the most important lessons that I want you to take away from this section and this entire book. The more effective you are in communicating the attributes that make you, a product, worth buying, the more value you will create for your brand, and the stronger impression you leave with others. Start to craft your elevator speech today and begin taking an inventory of your personal brand ambassadors. They will help you promote your brand so that you are not the only one working on your behalf and that your thirty-second commercial is one worth watching.

The way you communicate your personal brand attributes has a direct effect on the perception that others create about your value.

Chapter 6K

Know How to Create Your Own Opportunities

In This Chapter

- Creating opportunities
- Problems you can be known for solving
- Current reality vs. desired future state
- Thirty-Sixty-Ninety Day Plan

To succeed, jump as quickly at opportunities as you do at conclusions.

-Benjamin Franklin

We often think about opportunity as something we meet, win, stumble upon, miss out on or something that just plain happens to us over time. Opportunity, however, is obtained through focus, energy, effort, and planning. Building your personal brand is really about positioning yourself to gain opportunity. In other words, positioning yourself to achieve an intended goal through focus, effort, energy, and planning.

The goal of this chapter is to get you to think about how to create opportunities and to use them in a way that strengthens the attributes of your personal brand. Knowing how to create your own opportunities in life, business, and for your career is an important element in establishing your personal brand identity. When you are able to create your own opportunities you rely less on waiting for the things you cannot control to happen in your favor. This perspective allows you to direct your focus to what I call "controllable solutions to success." So let's explore five ways to create your own opportunities.

1. Know and uncover the problems you can be known for solving.

What is the strategic mission of your present employer or the employer you are looking to get a job from?

____

____

____

____

What does this company or organization want to be?

____

____

____

____

The first step in creating opportunities for yourself is to know how you can become an asset. In other words, what is it that you do to create value? Many of us have a job or career, but struggle to articulate what it is we actually do. This may be in part because we have not positioned ourselves in the context of the business value that our work achieves.

As a part of my self evaluation, I always try to ask myself if I am an expense or an asset. Understanding your value will help you better position yourself in the context of what your organization or company is trying to achieve. That is why it is so important to know the strategic mission of your employer. What better way to find out how you can be an asset than to know and uncover the problems you can be known for solving?

Think for a second about your capabilities, the skills and achievements that you bring to a problem situation. Are you known today for the things that you make better? Write your response to the questions on the lines below.

What are three problems that you want to be known for solving?

1. ____
2. ____
3. ____

Now write down the three words that describe the impression you want to leave with others.

1. ______________________________

2. ______________________________

3. ______________________________

Is there a correlation between the problems you can be known for solving and the impression you leave with others? Ideally, there should be a direct connection between the six words you have listed above. Your personal brand and the perception you create with others is a direct statement of your brand value. Often, your ability to be known for solving problems stems as much from your personal brand as from any technical skill you may have acquired. So how can you use this knowledge to create greater opportunities for yourself?

In the elevator example I referenced in chapter 5K, I created an opportunity by getting up from my desk and putting myself in the path of a chance encounter. I was able to *focus* on a goal of making sure I met the national marketing director before he left town. I took quite an *effort* to go to a high security floor of the building and walk around aimlessly, knowing that I might fail in my attempt and in the process run into opposition for being on the floor. My *energy* walking the floor with a piece of paper conveyed a sense of purpose, which masked the real ambiguity of the situation. And finally, because I had a *planned* elevator speech, I was prepared when the opportunity presented itself in that elevator ride.

Opportunity and preparation help eliminate outcomes that happen by chance. That "not-so chance" encounter led to a dream job. So my question to you, as you continue to read the 10Ks, what is it that you can do today to put yourself in the way of an opportunity?

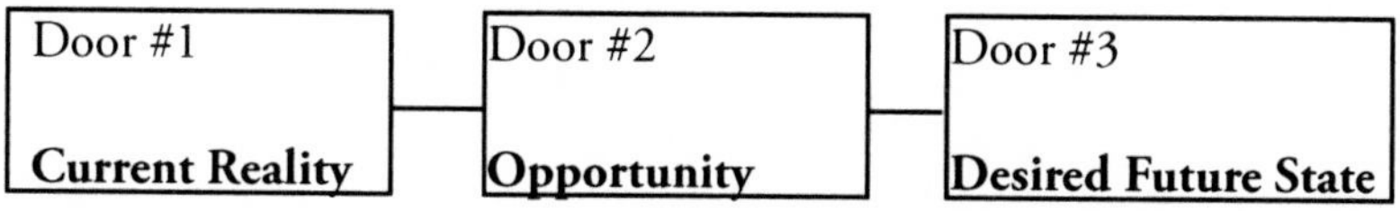

2. Continually assess your "current reality" and your "desired future state."

There is a common saying, "opportunity knocks." I say, opportunity lies behind what I call "door number two." In anything that we are faced with in life, I believe there are three doors that we eventually walk through.

Door Number One

This door represents your current state. I equate this to the state of your life right now, the condition of your being, and the trajectory of your career or professional aspirations. Door number one is where most people find themselves and also where most people stay for the better part of their lives.

Door Number Two

Door number two represents opportunity. It is where those that dare to focus with effort, energy, and planning find themselves at the end of a sometimes long journey. Door number two is the work that we do day in and day out. It is the sacrifices we make for ourselves, our family, and our loved ones, so that they will have the ability to dream and have those dreams come true. This door is also where we find the most casualties from the pursuit of success. In trying to go through door number two we sometimes fight against generations of historical failure that have kept those who came before us from ever seeing the fruits of their labor, the destination of where they wanted to be.

When I think about door number two, I think about my parents. They immigrated to the United States from the Caribbean with nothing but five children and a dream. Their only goal was for their children to one day have the opportunities that they would never see or think possible. I watched my dad work the 8 AM – 6 PM shift as a shipping clerk, and my mom work the 3 PM – 11 PM and 12 AM – 6 AM shifts as a nursing assistant. They sacrificed their body, sleep, health, wealth potential, friendships, and relationship with each other to drive a wedge that could crack door number two open. Door number two is where we win or lose. It is where we gain the courage to keep going or where we end up giving up.

Before we explore door number three I just want to share an original poem that I dedicate to my parents for their toil and their focus in helping me to see and believe that a door number two could be opened; and a door number three is something I could attain. I titled the poem "Inspiration," which is also the name I have chosen as my personal brand.

Inspiration

Kaplan Mobray

Live your legacy. Let be what is not what could be. Don't wait for tomorrow. Be ready today. Set the "go" in goals. Know the "know" in knowledge. Find the "free" in freedom. Lose the "me" in mediocrity. Accelerate the rate of advancement. Reject the acceptance of self doubt. Celebrate the you, you know you are. Or the you, you want to become. What holds you back are the dreams you have not had the courage to pursue. Are you enslaved by your own lack of ambition? Jailed by your own master? Locked by your own key? Or do you truly accept the responsibility to take your life and career forward? Are you on the runway to the destination of your dreams? Or are the minutes you live each day being wasted like un-recycled paper?

Thank you for reading this tribute. I hope it can inspire you to take yourself to new places. Even if that new place is the room next door.

Door Number Three

Door number three represents your desired future state. This is where we ultimately want to be as we continue to live our life and build our career. Having a clear focus on our desired future state helps us recognize when the opportunity presents itself to get us there. Door number three is where opportunity and preparation finally meet after a long hours, months, or years of being separated.

Opportunity and preparation get us to our desired future state and when we arrive there we realize that our personal brand was the guide that carried us through each door. You can always create opportunity somewhere between your "current reality" and your "desired future state," you just have to know that opportunity is behind door number two and that your personal brand is the guide to direct your footsteps.

You may see this as a simplistic way to view life in the context of opportunities. It is, but it is a method that will help you to put your present and your future in the context of creating a better and more improved "you." Each day take a view of your current reality and the desired future state of your present situation. Begin to see the opportunity that exists between these points. Your personal brand is an extension of the opportunities you create for yourself, and opportunities present themselves as a result of your personal brand. So where is your door number two? And what is standing between you and the outcomes you want for your life?

The Thirty-Sixty-Ninety Day Plan

Let's examine an effective way to open the door to opportunity. I call it the Thirty-Sixty-Ninety Day Personal Brand Plan.

STEP One
Thirty-day Aided Awareness Plan (Days 1 – 30)

Take thirty days and pick a routine in your life or career that you will change. For example, if you are used to wearing a shirt and pants to work, wear a suit for thirty days. If you are used to sitting in the back of the room, sit in the front. If you are always ten minutes late start being twenty minutes early. If you never say a word in meetings or group conversation prepare yourself to contribute in every meeting. Whatever the case, pick a routine that is visible to you and those who encounter you on a daily basis.

The goal of this exercise is to begin to raise your aided awareness. In other words get people to notice something new and fresh about you. You will be surprised at the reactions and the energy you will attract just by maintaining consistency in your new portrayal of yourself and breaking the consistency of your old norms. Do this for thirty days.

Now let's write down what you will do so you have a written commitment to refer back to daily.

What is it that you will do or change about yourself over the next thirty days?

____

____

____

____

The goal of this exercise is not to change your being but rather to transform your outlook. One of the most effective ways to transform your outlook is to incorporate a new and living perspective into what and who you will become. In other words, start focusing beyond your "being" and on your "becoming."

For example, if you see yourself as a leader but never get the opportunity to lead, start being the leader of your life, "the CEO of you" and the president of "Me, Inc." Make decisions for your life as if you were a CEO. Dress yourself as if you were chairman of your board. Give yourself daily updates on your progress and quarterly and annual reviews. You will be amazed at the focus you now have on creating what I call "selfholder value" and your ability to now see yourself as a true leader.

As you use this approach, focus on how it will extend to the other parts of your life and you will begin to be seen through the new outlook you have just created. After you have created aided awareness and have taken the thirty-day challenge, the next step is to use your new awareness to demonstrate capability.

STEP Two
Thirty-Days of Demonstration (Days 30 – 60)

Let's go back to the three problems you can be known for solving that you listed earlier in the chapter. How often and to whom do you demonstrate this problem solving? Take the next 30 days to focus on demonstrating your ability to solve the problems you identified as your defining capabilities. You can do this by setting up "planned demonstrations of your brand." Let me explain this further.

Have you ever gone to a rally where protesters have planned a demonstration for a cause? What is your initial perception of these events? For some, it's easy to turn your back at protest events and scorn those who set up demonstrations for a cause. After all, it's not everyday that you see a large number of volunteers who willingly put their life on the line in some form of physical demonstration of opposition. And in some cases you may not agree with the cause for demonstration. For others you understand that protest is a form of progress and a demonstration is a visible way to create the foundation for forward movement on an issue.

A demonstration is an effective way to influence action and a means to send a strong message. Similarly, when it comes to your personal brand, setting up a planned demonstration is an effective way to influence action and to send a strong message as to who you are and what you are capable of achieving. Many of us, however, have rarely organized our own personal brand demonstration. I would argue that we have attended many brand demonstrations held by others perhaps without even knowing it.

So let's explore an approach to setting up your own personal brand demonstration. The key is to focus your demonstration to create an actionable display of capability. Here's a demonstration you can try out for yourself.

A. Select ten things that you are going to get done in the next thirty days. It could be:

- Ten problems you are going to solve
- Ten ways that you are going to create a positive outcome
- Ten questions you are going to provide answers to
- Ten new projects you are going to start

B. The next step is to identify ten individuals you will ask to send a message to your supervisor or someone you want to impress praising the great work you did or the accomplishments you are making. By doing this, you are launching a deliberate demonstration of your capability using messengers to rally for your personal brand.

There is a delicate balance between being deliberate and being genuine when promoting your brand. If you are too deliberate you may not come off as genuine, and if you are too genuine you may not be deliberate enough in the delivery of your message, and it loses impact. To succeed at this step, ask your brand ambassadors to send correspondence to your manager, supervisor, or the person you want to impress using an electronic medium like e-mail. E-mail removes the emotion connected with being too genuine and generally enhances the nature of formal requests to be more deliberate in tone. In addition, this step requires that you base the request for your brand ambassadors to share the good word of you out of an inclination to help others. Helping others always leads to positive reinforcement of your personal brand.

C. Finally, map your personal brand rallies on a calendar so you have a balanced approach over this thirty day demonstration period. For those who have the courage to embrace an actionable way to achieve immediate results in building your personal brand, this demonstration is for you. It has worked for me and many others who I have counseled and I encourage you to use it to create your own positive outcomes.

The key to making this work is being deliberate in engaging the individual messengers, (brand ambassadors), who will champion your efforts and help you to showcase your capability. The greater the number of individual sources the more effective your personal brand demonstration. So let's write it down so you can refer back to this demonstration later.

My Personal Brand Demonstration
Ten things I am going to get done in the next thirty days.

1. ______________________________

2. ______________________________

3. ______________________________

4. ________________________________

5. ________________________________

6. ________________________________

7. ________________________________

8. ________________________________

9. ________________________________

10. ________________________________

Ten individual brand ambassadors who will endorse the great work or accomplishments I produce.

1. Name________________________________
2. Name________________________________
3. Name________________________________
4. Name________________________________
5. Name________________________________
6. Name________________________________
7. Name________________________________
8. Name________________________________
9. Name________________________________
10. Name________________________________

Personal Brand demonstration calendar	Number of demonstrations
Day 1 – 10	3
Day 11 – 20	4
Day 21 – 30	3

Having mastered the thirty and sixty day plan, you are now ready for the ninety day personal brand drive.

STEP Three
Thirty Day Personal Brand Drive (Days 60 – 90)

Have you ever gone to a blood drive in your local office or community center? These are among the most effective volunteer donor programs today. In short, you have volunteers willing to donate a vital component of what keeps them alive to help save others. On top of this, each donor is able to connect with others who have the same blood type, creating a new network of type O negatives, type As, and type Bs who share the same values and pride of blood donorship. This network also can create new opportunities for social interaction and professional networking, and restores one's commitment to return next year as a donor. But have you ever held a brand drive for your personal brand? Have you ever volunteered to donate the success of your brand to help save others?

The last leg of the thirty-sixty-ninety day plan is your personal brand drive. This volunteer effort will help you put into action the capabilities you have developed through your personal brand to show results and save others. It will also help you to build your network among similar personal brand types to create new opportunities for networking, social interaction, and a commitment to continue to help others. So let's explore an approach for your ninety day personal brand drive.

In thirty days you have created aided awareness for yourself, and in sixty days you have launched proactive demonstrations of your personal brand. Now it's time to let the results speak through your personal brand drive. The first step is to set up your own personal brand center. This is a place or vehicle you will use to donate your capabilities to help others. For many of us who work in large corporate settings this venue is the company or department newsletter. For others, this venue could be the weekly team meeting, the fifteen minute coffee break, the 10 AM status update call, the 12:30 group lunch outing, the 3 PM snack break, or whatever consistent venue you find that enables you to be among others you can help. Use this time to donate lessons learned in your personal brand transformation.

So let's take the fifteen minute coffee run, whenever this may occur during your day. Pick someone each day to share one element of how you have begun to transform your personal brand. Ask them if they have a routine in their personal or professional life that they would like to change. Share with them your thirty day aided awareness plan and the results you were able to achieve in your sixty day demonstration.

What you will find is that you begin to brand yourself as someone genuinely interested in helping others, and at the same time open up opportunities to further spread your personal brand and increase its value. The more personal brand drives you set up, the larger the community you build in support of personal brand fulfillment.

I know for some of you this may sound a little preachy. And in some cases it may not be natural or comfortable to approach others in this manner. Just as it may feel when you are approached to give blood or donate to a specific charity. The point of this approach is to give back and share your examples of personal brand fulfillment that can help others in their own journey to achieve personal enrichment.

Another approach to this is to get a "10K buddy." Your buddy is someone who you will share the 10Ks with and discuss one of the "K's" each week as you work together to build your personal brand. This is an effective way to use this book. My goal is to get you to manage the external perceptions you create with others through an intimate understanding of your personal brand. Practicing these principles and getting feedback from a buddy along the way will accelerate your personal brand development. Are you ready for the thirty-sixty-ninety day personal brand challenge?

3. Mind the gap

Another way to create your own opportunities is to what I call "mind the gap." If you have ever traveled to England and taken the loop metro train you may be familiar with the phrase "mind the gap." In that instance, the gap represents danger, because if you step out of the train and into the gap you are likely to fall or be crushed. As it relates to your personal brand, this gap is "where you live." You are not likely to fall or be thrown off course if you live in the gap between your current state and your desired future state.

Let's dig a little deeper on this one. This is where a mirror will come in handy. If you are not near a mirror then look out at something that will allow you to peacefully reflect. Start by asking yourself some tough questions.

What is the current reality of your life? Think about your personal or professional situation as it exists right now and write a response on the lines below.

____

____

____

____

Are you happy with yourself? The "you" you see in the mirror?

____

If you could change one thing about you what would that be?

____

What concrete outcome do you want to achieve for yourself in life?

____

What are the forces that prevent you from achieving them?

____

Now reflect a moment on the realistic opportunities that would allow you to touch the positive outcomes you strive for. Write them down on the lines below.

____

____

____

____

Now let's go back to the three words you wrote down earlier that describe the impression you want to leave with others.

1. ______________

2. ______________

3. ______________

How do your answers to the tough questions above relate to the impression you leave with others? How does this impression help you create opportunities for yourself?

By analyzing situations in this context, you begin to shift the focus of your existence to a continual state of self-improvement. More importantly, this continual state of self-improvement will help you seek out positive outcomes without fear and accept challenges as mere opportunities. It will also give you more courage to take risks by implementing "fixes" to the gaps between your current reality and your desired future state. As we discussed earlier, there is great value in taking risks.

4. Leave home

Another way to create your own opportunity is to "leave home." By leaving home, I mean get involved with areas, events, and activities outside your day-to-day responsibilities. This will help you to expand your network, expose you to opportunities to establish relationships, and share your personal brand. It also gives you the freedom to demonstrate your capabilities in other ways. Let's explore this further:

What is your day-to-day occupation?

____

What are the outside recreational or professional activities and events that you participate in?

____

____

____

____

What are the capabilities that you demonstrate through these outside activities?

____

____

____

____

Again, write down the three words you wish to leave as your lasting impression with others.

1. ____________________
2. ____________________
3. ____________________

Can you see similarities in your personal brand attributes and the opportunities you create for yourself through outside involvement? When you begin to take an external view of your life activities and their correlation to the lasting impression you leave with others, you will start to clearly see just how your personal brand gets established. You will also begin to see the external opportunities you can use to further demonstrate your capabilities. Here's an example.

Par-Man

I have a friend who is an avid golfer. His love for the game stems not from his ability to drive the ball far or putt from long range. He enjoys the mathematical challenge of measuring distances to the hole. So much so, that he will hit many shots with less distance just for the opportunity to measure (in his head) feet and yards away from the hole divided by incline and wind resistance. I know what you're saying. What person has more fun doing the math related to golf than hitting the ball in the small round hole? Let me tell you more about my friend.

Through his golf habit, which some now call an addiction, he became pretty good at measuring the risk associated with being two hundred fifty yards away on a par three hole. After a while he became so good that he made a name for himself at his local club for predicting player's stroke count per hole. He predicted that an average golfer, on a two hundred fifty yard par-three hole, would hit the ball one hundred twenty yards in the first stroke, one hundred yards in the second stroke, with an average wind speed of five miles per hour, leaving themselves open for a thirty foot putt that they could make in two strokes. Further, he predicted that as the average wind speed increased by five miles per hour it would result in an end distance to the cup decreased by five feet.

Well, I thought he was crazy, as you probably do right now, but his passion for calculating this formula could not be contained. So we began calling him "Par-man." Par-man became his personal brand, one that he embraced and wore with pride. Everywhere he went he would hear folks say "What's up Par-man?" He even had t-shirts made with his famed name. Well, Par-man's day job was an automobile salesman, and while he enjoyed selling cars, he really did not get to use his passion for simulating mathematical outcomes based on distance and wind speed.

One day, he saw an ad for a job as a research manager with a life insurance company. He knew on the surface that there was no correlation between selling automobiles and deciding how to give life insurance coverage, but he went for it anyway with the hope that he would get some interview practice.

In his interview he spent much of his time talking about golf. He mentioned how predicting stroke counts based on an analysis of distance and wind speed is just like selling insurance. He mentioned that his skill for golf could easily be replicated in helping a company develop a predictive model for providing insurance coverage. After nearly forty-five minutes of conversation and sharing examples of his analytical skills and how he successfully predicted stroke counts on the golf course, he was offered the job. Years later, Par-man went on to become the head of risk management for a leading insurance provider. He also was finally able to shed his pet name. His new name became "boss."

This is just one example of how a personal passion, tied to a personal brand, created a positive opportunity. What's your story? What's your passion and how can you use it to create opportunities for your life and career? Personal branding is really about positioning yourself to create opportunities to succeed. So you can conclude that creating a better you starts with creating a better personal brand. As you think about the steps you have taken or need to take to begin living your desired future state, think about the game plan to get there. There is a road to success; I hope that this chapter will help you avoid one extra stop for directions.

We often think about opportunity as something we meet, win, stumble upon, miss out on, or something that just plain happens to us over time. Opportunity however, is obtained through focus, energy, effort, and planning.

Chapter 7K

Know and Master the Art of Connection

In This Chapter

- Networking
- Connecting traits with people
- Learning how to small talk in a positive way
- How to be a connector
- Connecting ideas and people

Networking is an effective tool in driving business growth and professional success. It is something that you do in some form each and every day you come in contact with others. However, most of us do not maximize the value of our social and professional networks and thus diminish opportunities for our personal brand to shine. This chapter will focus on how to master the art of connection to help you become better at networking and help you establish stronger connections with the people you encounter.

Networking

Have you ever attempted to network with someone and after your first attempt to break the ice with idle conversation you decide you really don't need to know that person? You walk away feeling that there's nothing to be gained from a conversation, so you cut the conversation and your interaction short. Then, months later you are applying for a job or asking for something that could lead to opportunity and that very same person is someone you will now have to impress? Has this ever happened to you?

This scenario happens often, and I would bet at some point in your life it has or will happen to you. What enables you to be on the favorable end of this situation is your ability to make a positive and memorable connection with those you encounter. You never know who you will meet along the way and the impression you leave with others. Sometimes, you make an impression by having a memorable story to tell, greeting someone with a memorable smile, wearing a memorable article of clothing, or introducing someone to a new way of thinking. The point is conversations and interactions create opportunity.

Think about the last time you connected with someone in the context of networking. What conversation topics did you use to start your interaction? Did you have a game plan or approach to how you would connect with others? Was there a specific goal that you wanted to achieve from the networking encounter? The reality is many of us struggle to make meaningful connections with others, especially those we want to impress, simply because we do not know how to engage a conversation.

Having a formula for making connections gives you an approach that you can be comfortable with and master over time. We often don't think about how we start a conversation, or the conversation topics we will use to connect with others, but having an approach and game plan is what drives success from networking opportunities and what will help you establish a meaningful connection with others. So to be effective at networking, start by deciding what you will use as your conversation starter in any interaction. Here are a sample of conversation starters and questions that naturally come up in the context of meeting someone for the first time.

Conversation Starters

What is your name?
Where do you live?
Where did you and your family grow up?
What do you do as an occupation?
What did you do in the past, prior to this occupation?
How long have you been in that role?
How long have you been at your company?
What's your favorite baseball team?
Have you traveled recently to anywhere exciting?
What are some of your favorite foods?

These questions may sound a bit obvious, but as I mentioned, many of us struggle to make meaningful connections with others, especially those we want to impress simply because we do not have a specific formula for engaging a conversation.

The conversation starter questions above will allow you to get to know the people with whom you interact. As you share more about yourself and learn more about others, you begin to build the lasting and memorable connections that over time open the doors to opportunity and enrich your life.

So let's explore the art of making a connection. Not just any connection though, a meaningful connection so that you become memorable, positively impressionable, and build an unforgettable personal brand.

Have you ever played the board game Connect Four? Do you know anyone who is good at this game? What are the reasons you win? Most people who are good at Connect Four are good because they have an ability to see and make quick connections to matching elements. Similarly, the more you can connect with someone, the more likely you will leave a memorable impression. Personal branding is about leaving a memorable impression. It is how you create a distinct impression that allows you to be remembered and your capabilities noticed, so that you can realize greater opportunities and success.

Connecting With Others (The Game Plan)

Think for a second about how you connect with others. Do you have a specific style or approach that guides your interactions? What are the actions and behaviors that allow you to gain entry to someone you have met for the first time?

We often think about networking as something that happens in a room by virtue of chance encounters and idle conversation. But, the best networkers, those who master the art of connection, actually have a game plan for interacting with others long before they enter any room or networking situation. So let's explore the art of making a connection. Not just any connection, though. We are looking for a meaningful connection so that you become memorable, positively impressionable, and build an unforgettable personal brand.

The Five Dimensions of Connection

There are five dimensions that determine the connection you make with another. The stronger your mastery of each dimension, the stronger the connection you build with those you encounter. They include:

1. **Physical connection** (appearance, greeting gesture)
2. **Signal connection** (eye contact, facial expression, posture)
3. **Emotional connection** (emotional, beliefs, outlook)

4. **Verbal connection** (tone of voice, conversation rhythm, enthusiasm)
5. **Experience connection** (past experience, trigger event, shared moment or activity)

Let's explore each dimension in detail and outline specific actions that you can do to maximize your networking and connection effectiveness.

1. Physical Connection

Your physical connection represents the connection you establish with others through your personal appearance and greeting gesture. It is a widely held belief that people gravitate toward people they are attracted to. Several psychological studies have confirmed this theory and also confirm that physical attraction is among the strongest dimensions of how we connect with others. According to Yale University psychology professor Marianne LaFrance, in her contributing article for Lamas Beauty Magazine titled *First Impressions and Hair Impressions*, she notes that ninety percent of a first impression is based on appearance, posture, facial expressions, and tone of voice.

Physical connection derives from your personal appearance or "good looks," and is enhanced by your greeting gesture when engaging with others. Your personal appearance and greeting gesture are often the first set of attributes that allow you to garner attention and create an impression where others will want to connect with you. Your personal brand is enhanced, and often defined, by these physical attributes, so it is important to be conscious of them when attempting to create a connection with others. Here are some ways to use the physical connection dimension to establish better connections as you meet and network with others.

Step One

Before entering any room decide how you will use your personal appearance as a way to connect with others. Recognize what your personal appearance says about you.

When I prepare for a networking event or an opportunity where I will meet someone for the first time, I often make it a point to wear a distinctive tie or article of clothing. I do this because I want to establish a strong impression about my personal brand through my personal appearance and have a ready-to-use conversation piece for engaging a conversation. So for example, when I hear "nice tie" or when you may hear "nice shoes," it opens the door for a "thank you," which is a nice way to ease into connecting with someone. Think about the last time someone complimented you at the start of a conversation. Was it easier after that instance to engage in meaningful dialogue?

Now, I am not saying that you should always look for compliments; you could also be the one complimenting the new contact you just made. If it turns out that you entered a room where everyone is wearing black and you are wearing red, instead of making yourself the odd one out, be proactive and create a story that connects your personal appearance to an impression you deliberately want to make or drive in the minds of others.

For example, I recall a time when I was at a business networking event where several executives were being honored. The event was mostly a sea of navy blue suits, white shirts, and red ties. Anyone who wore something other than that combination truly stood out. As the room continued to fill up with guests, I noticed a particular gentleman who wore a pink bow tie along with a gray suit and sharp thin-rimmed glasses. He clearly stood out, and although he had on a suit, he did not seem to fit the mold of the majority of executives in the room.

I made my way over to strike up a conversation with him mainly so I could find out who he was and what he did for a living. I thought for a second that he may be an actor or someone famous who was trying to remain anonymous. I went over to him, introduced myself and said, "nice tie." He thanked me, and then told me that he was wearing it in honor of a breast cancer awareness event taking place the following week.

I smiled for a second and mentioned to him that I was signed up to take part in an event for breast cancer awareness in the coming week too, and wondered if it was the same event. He replied, "Great, I'll see you there." The following week I attended the breast cancer event only to find out that the gentleman who I had met a week prior was the chairman of the foundation sponsoring the event. He quickly remembered me and introduced me to several others on his board. I connected with them throughout the night and went on to stay in touch with several of the business partners on the foundation in the months ahead. A year later I joined his board and have been an active member in helping to raise money for several cause-related initiatives ever since. When I think back to how this connection started, it all began with two words: "nice tie."

The point I want to emphasize is that how you use your personal appearance to get noticed is a great tool to establish strong connections and favorable impressions for your personal brand. And, when used proactively, it can lead to opportunities and advancement.

As you think about your own personal appearance, make a conscious choice about what you want your personal appearance to say about you. Also, be conscious of the appearance of those you meet, use details and genuine compliments to drive conversation starters. It will be your first line of offense in building a connection with others through networking.

Step Two

Select a greeting gesture that conveys your personality and your intention.

Are you a hugger? How firm is your handshake? And when is it okay to give a high five?

The way you greet someone will tell a lot about your personal brand. People connect based on how they greet each other, and as a result, your greeting gesture will determine the strength of your connection with others.

Huggers

Do you notice the people who hug upon greeting someone? I call them "huggers." Typically, huggers convey through their greeting gesture that they are open, warm, affectionate, and accepting. This gesture gives the people they meet the permission to establish a closer connection with them and creates a forum for a deeper level of sharing or receiving of information. Huggers may also gain a deeper level of trust and eventual sponsorship as they connect with others. A hug is not just a physical embrace but it is also an embrace of your personal brand. When used wisely, it can be an effective tool to establish a meaningful connection.

Let's Shake On It

On the flip side, not everyone is a hugger and not everyone is comfortable being hugged. The more standard and most accepted greeting gesture when encountering someone is the handshake.

According to Peter M. Hall and Dee Ann Hall in "The Handshake as Interaction," the origin of the handshake dates back to medieval Europe when kings and knights would extend their hands to each other, and grasp the other's hand as a demonstration that each did not possess concealed weapons and intended no harm to the other.[8] This definition of the handshake most closely resembles our use of the handshake today as a way to introduce ourselves to a person and open ourselves up to them for the purpose of interacting. Interestingly enough, the ancient Greeks used it similarly as a welcoming sign of friendliness, hospitality, and trust.[9]

Mover and Shaker

In business, a handshake opens and closes a deal. It is considered a promissory note, or a receipt of payment. We often do not pay attention to our handshake, but how you shake can actually shape the impression you create with others and the perception of your personal brand. Here are some tips on handshakes. I won't call them the art of the handshake, but you can bet if you master these tips you will be on your way to becoming a mover and a "shaker."

Firm Handshake

A firm handshake conveys confidence and focused energy. This greeting gesture is best used in a business networking setting, job interview, or meeting someone for the first time. In business, a firm handshake is important because it is a symbol of a relationship. According to Ivan R. Misner, coauthor of *Masters of Sales* and the Web site Entrepreneur.com, seventy percent of business transactions are done on the basis of relationships and referrals. This means that even if you have the best product or service, you may lose the opportunity if someone else has a stronger relationship with the buyer. Whether you are entering into a new relationship, solidifying an existing relationship, or ending a relationship transaction, a firm handshake is a strong symbol of your word. Because of this a firm handshake is best used when creating opportunity or gain, especially in a business setting. So let's break down what makes a firm handshake.

Breaking Down the "Shake"

For best results, use what I call the "**C**atch-**P**ump-**R**elease (CPR)" method.

1. Establish eye contact
2. Hold hand out at a ninety degree angle with your thumb pointing straight up
3. Catch and interlock hands so that your thumbs are parallel and the area between your thumbs and index fingers are concealed
4. Pump or shake hands twice starting in an upwards direction and then downward so that you create a rhythm (up down, up down)
5. Bring your body forward in direction of person you are greeting
6. Release your hand and maintain eye contact as you disengage from the shake

Mild Handshake

A mild handshake conveys a more casual and subdued nature. It is best used in settings where there is no direct pressure of performance or evaluation. The mild shake is the most common of the shakes and is what the average person will default to for the everyday encounter. It is characterized by the goal of establishing a casual relationship or engaging someone as part of a casual greeting encounter.

As I mentioned, a mild shake is appropriate when there is no direct pressure of performance or evaluation. This is an important fact to grasp, because if you give too firm a handshake in a more casual encounter, it can drive more negative impressions about your brand. Let's break down the mild handshake to illustrate this method.

For best results:

1. Establish eye contact
2. Hold your hand out at a forty-five degree angle with your thumb pointing slightly forward to down
3. Catch and interlock hands so that your thumbs are parallel and the area between both thumbs and index fingers is concealed
4. Pump or shake hands twice starting in downward direction and then upward so that you create a rhythm (down up, down up)
5. Bring your body forward in the direction of the person you are greeting
6. Release your hand and maintain eye contact as you disengage from the shake

Limp Handshake

A limp handshake also called the "fish" handshake is the least common and least desirable of all the shakes. A limp handshake conveys a variety of negative attributes that may lessen the value of your personal brand. It conveys a lack of confidence, low self-esteem, disdain or disgust, and a reservation that you may be unsure of yourself or the product or service you are selling. It is to be avoided at all times unless you are deliberately trying to convey disinterest, disdain, disgust, or simply want to disengage from the person you are speaking with.

Think about the last time you either gave or received a limp handshake. If you are like most people, you probably drew some strong conclusions about the person giving the limp handshake or were disappointed in the person for giving it to you. If you are the recipient of a limp handshake, stop and think about your connection to the person. Often people give limp handshakes to send a message that they are disinterested in connecting with you. We often don't read the signs and thus these hand signals go right over our head.

Regardless of the "hand" you are dealt, limp handshakes are less effective in establishing a strong connection and will make you less credible in a business networking setting. It is, however, an effective signal to distance yourself from the people you do not want to connect with in any meaningful way. If your intention is to deliberately give a limp handshake, then follow the example below.

The **P**ick-**T**ips-**D**rop (PTD) method:

1. Establish eye contact
2. Hold your hand out at forty-five degree angle downward with palm closed and fingers in a pick-up position
3. Pick up the other person's fingertips, keeping your palm semi-closed so that there is no opportunity for the space between your thumbs and index fingers to connect.
4. Pump hands once starting in upward direction then downward direction so that you create one rhythm (up down)
5. Maintain body stance with a slight movement backwards in the opposite direction of person you are greeting
6. Release your hand and maintain short eye contact as you disengage from the shake

As you can see, the limp handshake is not the most desirable to give or receive. It is thus important to be aware of the type of messages you may be sending just based on this greeting gesture.

Mastering the Art of Hand-to-Hand Connections

Your greeting gesture may impact the connections you make with others. So take a couple of minutes and think about your handshake greeting or hug gesture and what they may indicate about you. As you begin to become more aware of your greeting gesture and your style for engaging others, you will realize that people will make assumptions of your value just based on how you greet them. This means that you could miss out on opportunities before ever having a chance to verbalize your value.

So to master the art of connection, I want you to do an exercise that will help you raise your awareness of your greeting gesture and the perception you have of others as they greet you.

Exercise

1. Randomly pick ten people and make a plan to shake their hand or give them a hug greeting as you would normally do
2. Make a mental note of how they shake your hand in the interaction
3. Return to an area where you can record your observations and write on a pad three words that you would use to describe each person based on their handshake or hug greeting gesture.
4. Divide your list of people into huggers and shakers and segment by firm, mild, and limp handshakes
5. When you look at your list, reflect on which people came across more confident, which were more uncertain of themselves, and record which people you connected with the most
6. Finally, if you were to award one person on your list a one-hundred thousand dollar reward, write down the one person's name to whom you would award this prize

This exercise should yield some very interesting findings and some surprises. My hope is that it makes you more aware of the impact your greeting gesture will have on your ability to establish meaningful connections.

Signal Connection

Your signal connection is the connection you establish through nonverbal communication. You make this connection most commonly through your eye contact, facial expression, and your posture when meeting or engaging others.

According to a 1968 study by A. Mehrabian in *Psychology Today*, only seven percent of an initial impression is based on what's said. Thirty-eight percent is based on style of speech and fifty-five percent on body language. The same study suggests that nonverbal cues are more important to *understanding and believing* communication than the words themselves. In fact, there's an entire language form based on this phenomena. They call it sarcasm!

The point is, nonverbal communication, or what I call "signals," have a direct impact on how and why we connect with others. This includes eye contact, facial expression, and posture. To master the art of connection, you must have an understanding of how to use your signals to create a connection and make a compelling impression on others.

Eye Contact

One of the biggest myths about eye contact is that others don't see what you see. What I mean by this is that we often underestimate what our eyes say about us and how easy it is for others to comprehend how we feel just by looking at our eyes. The reality is your eyes tell all. They convey confidence, expose uncertainty, state your case, and reveal the result of something you may try to hide. When meeting someone for the first time or in a networking situation, focus on what your eyes say about your encounter. Eyes first gravitate to one's personal appearance, then facial expressions, and then posture, after which the brain does an appraisal and computes a value of your worth. All of this before you even say one word. The eyes are very powerful tools in establishing connections with others. So here are a couple of tips on how to use your eyes to drive connection.

Direct Eye-to-Eye Contact

When you greet someone, look directly into their eyes as you extend your hand for a handshake or open your arms for a hug. This is a simple thing, but you would be surprised to know that most people have a phobia of looking someone directly in the eyes.

Direct eye contact upon meeting someone conveys confidence and an intent to connect. If you avoid direct eye contact or look down when greeting someone, you may send a signal that you are not interested in connecting with that person or lack self-confidence, which will create a lesser impression of your value.

The Triangle Stare

After you have established direct eye contact through your greeting gesture, you will have conveyed your interest in connecting with the other person and communicated a confidence about you that signifies your value. Direct eye contact, however, is not something that you need to carry out for an entire conversation.

It is neither natural nor comfortable to maintain direct eye-to-eye contact throughout an entire conversation, unless you are being officially interrogated. So how do you keep a focus on the connection you are establishing with someone without creating the wrong impression through a prolonged period of direct eye-to-eye contact?

Your eyes are a great way to emphasize specific points you are making as part of a conversation. The natural rhythm of your eyes in a conversation is what engages others, helps convey interest, and sets the pace for your focus on the conversation. Another way to think about this is that your eyes pick up content then deposit the emphasis of what you are conveying into the eyes of the person with whom you are speaking.

There is a technique I call the triangle stare that will help you to become more comfortable with your eyes in a conversation. The triangle stare is a technique that will help you maintain your focus in a conversation, present yourself as being engaged in the discussion, and alleviate the pressure associated with prolonged direct eye-to-eye contact.

The next time you are in a conversation with someone, take notice of how long you stare directly into their eyes, how long you stare off to the right half of their face just above the cheek, and then the left half of their face just above the cheek. Whether you are conscious of this or not, it is a behavior you involuntarily elicit during a conversation. As you become more conscious of your eye contact during conversation you can master this technique and begin to use your eyes as a way to focus when connecting with someone through conversation.

- The triangle stare starts with direct eye contact for a focused period of time at the start of a conversation.
- As the conversation progresses, your eyes look slightly downward into the eye but from the vantage point above the right cheek
- Your eyes then move back into direct eye-to-eye contact position
- As the conversation progresses, your eyes look slightly downward into the eye but from the vantage point above the left cheek
- Your eyes then move back into the direct eye-to-eye contact position

The goal of the triangle stare is to remain focused, connected, and engaged in the conversation by not taking your eyes off the person you are speaking with in a manner that is comfortable and nonthreatening as you see eye-to-eye. With this level of focus, you will begin to have more meaningful conversations as you network with others and ultimately establish greater connections. Try it the next time you are engaged in conversation and see for yourself how you can master the art of connection through eye contact.

Posture is Power

Have you ever been in a crowded room and notice right away someone who walks in with extreme confidence in their posture? These are the people we notice, are intrigued by, and want to make sure we connect with before leaving the room.

The phenomenon behind this scenario, what I call, "the person who just entered the room," is that posture equals power. We often do not pay attention to our posture, but it is a strong form of communication. Your posture will communicate how confident you are in yourself, how prepared you are to engage others, and the level of success others will automatically associate with your personal brand.

Posture is most commonly stated as how you carry yourself. You may have heard someone say that they like the way someone carries themself. People often use this phrase to depict a person's style or approach to handling a host of situations. What they are really observing, however, is that person's posture.

Just like the other signal attributes we explored previously (facial expression and eye contact), people will make assumptions of your value based on your posture. They will seek to connect or reject you by observing how you carry yourself. What this means is that you may decrease your ability to connect with others and establish a meaningful connection just by having poor posture.

How you carry yourself will increase or decrease your likeability, your approachability, your connectability, and most importantly your personal brand appeal. So how do you carry yourself? And, what does your posture say about you?

The 3 Fs of Posture

There are three categories I use to describe the posture that most people exude:

1. **Frame**: The frame is a strong upright posture that commands attention. This posture connotes confidence, openness, and signifies success.

People with a strong frame postulate their success. In other words they use nonverbal signals to communicate their success and confidence. For many it is characterized by their personal appearance, their actual stance when in the presence of others, and their mindset which exudes a "rise above the issue" and "stay cool under pressure" mentality. People with a strong frame are recognizable and stand out prominently in a crowd. It is not surprising that many people who have assumed leadership roles or positions of authority, have celebrity status, or another level of prominence based on their achievements also have a strong frame. You may ask if the strong frame comes as a result of leadership and celebrity status. Or does one's strong frame make them an assumed leader or celebrity? Both views are accurate.

A strong frame increases your ability to establish meaningful connections by raising the awareness and appeal of your brand.

2. **Flop**: A slouchy posture, the flop is characterized by hunched over, shrugged shoulders and a reliance on external structures to hold you up that connotes a guarded existence, low self-esteem, and lack of ambition.

A flopped posture is just what it sounds like: a flop. People whose posture exudes a slouch, hunch, shrug, fold, and lean typically also have less confidence, less appeal, and less perceived value. Unlike the frame posture, you find fewer leaders, celebrities, and persons of authority who exude a flopped posture because by the very nature of the flop. It is not the most desirable characteristic to emulate or pattern. You will notice that people with a flop posture spend more time avoiding networking situations or opportunities and thus have less-known, less-established personal brands. As a result they are also less connected, have lower political capital within their organizations, and are among the last to be approached for opportunities for advancement or gain. If this depiction sounds in any way like your posture, know that your life and professional career outcomes will be limited by the very nature of your posture.

3. **Frozen:** This is a tightly wound posture characterized by arms crossed or folded to hold yourself in like a concealed weapon. This posture connotes fear, an aversion to risk, and that you are closed to possibilities of new or unplanned experiences.

People with what I call a frozen posture have strong nonverbal signals that deter others from engaging them. Among the strongest of these traits is a frown, or expressionless facial expression also known as a poker face. If you think about the people you know who always have a frown on their face, think about the other characteristics that you associate with that person. Often these are the people who we look to avoid, stay out of their way, or appease out of fear.

There are many leaders and persons of authority who exude a frozen posture. These are the leaders who most typically rule by instilling fear in the people around them as a means to elevate their value. I would argue that these types of leaders or persons have diminished value in their ability to connect with others in the long run and ultimately will have more negative perceptions and attributes associated with their personal brand. Do you know anyone with a frozen posture? As you analyze the characteristics of the 3 Fs, which posture category do you most identify with?

Posture Perfect

When you walk into a room, people will file you into a mental category based on your posture. You will be considered someone with a frame, a flop, or a frozen posture. This, combined with the other signal attributes, will create the impression that others take away as the value of your brand, which will result in the level of connection you are able to establish.

To develop a strong posture, focus on the way you enter a room and what you want it to say about you. This takes planning and preparation so you can carry yourself with the same consistent attributes you want to convey about your personal brand. Here are five tips to practice your posture when presenting yourself and positioning your personal brand:

1. **Stand and walk tall** – Practice walking tall with your head up, shoulders back, and chest out, as if you were a solid frame. The more natural and upright your posture, the more you are capable of conveying confidence
2. **Smile** – A smile attracts others to you and lets others know it is safe to engage you to establish a connection. A smile also conveys that you are comfortable with yourself which will make others comfortable with you.
3. **Center yourself** – When you walk into a crowded room, walk directly into the center of the room and remain there for a few minutes with your posture frame steady to take in the room. As you take in the room and assess who is present, others will take notice of the fact that you are present. As a result, you will build presence and begin to attract others to you, increasing your networking output and ability to connect with others.
4. **Spare the cross for praying hands** – If you are someone who always crosses your arms when speaking to someone, your posture may signal that you are closed off from listening, engaging, or connecting with others. This stance can ultimately send the wrong impression and limit you from opportunities without your knowing. Try opening up your posture using the praying hands stance.

Crossed arms

Praying hands

Praying hands actually connote thinking which is an admired trait within the context of a conversation. When people perceive you are thinking about what they are saying, they also believe you are listening. Active listening in the context of a thinking pose will engage you further in the conversation and help you establish a stronger connection with others as a result. The next time you watch a television show host, take notice of how they use their hands during the broadcast. You'll see the praying hands posture used in television as hosts are trying to connect with their viewing audience.

5. **Sit "UBU" Sit** – Your seated posture is just as important as your posture when standing or entering a room. Where you sit, how you sit, and ultimately how you project when seated will convey confidence and credibility allowing you to better connect with others. To maximize your seated posture I challenge you to use what I call the "Sit UBU Sit" methodology.

Sit UBU Sit was the popular closing tag for UBU productions, producer of hit shows like *Family Ties* (1982-1989) and *Spin City* (1996-2002). As it relates to your seated posture I refer to Sit UBU Sit as "**S**it **U**nder the **B**ig **U**mbrella Seat." When you enter a meeting room or space where several folks will be gathered, there is an invisible umbrella in the room. The center of the room or table is the umbrella handle and is where you have the strongest position to connect broadly with others. It is from this seated position that your posture projects for maximum exposure. You want to keep a strong upright seated frame when sitting in the center of a room or gathering. Just like with an umbrella, the further you are away from the handle the more likely you are to have less relevance because you are exposed to the elements. In this case, the elements represent those things that prevent you from being a focal part of a meeting or conversation. So always make an effort to seat yourself where you can gain solid exposure and attention, especially when you are sharing information or making a critical point in the context of a conversation.

It's also important to note that sometimes the umbrella is not in the center of the room, but represents the area where the person of most authority and influence is seated. When seating yourself in a meeting or gathering look to find who that person or persons are and create your umbrella directly across from them. You want to be able to establish eye contact during a conversation or meeting with these persons. The more you are in their line of sight the greater your ability to establish a connection and drive focused attention to the great things you have to convey in the meeting.

Emotional Connection

Your emotional connection is the connection you gain from engaging in dialogue that reveals your emotions, beliefs, or outlook on a particular subject matter. This type of connection is both powerful and lasting, making it one of the most effective dimensions on which to establish a solid connection with others.

When you speak to someone and realize that they share a common belief, position on an issue, or perspective on life, you in essence become "one" with that person. Further, in that instance of the conversation or moment in a room, you gain the respect of the person you are speaking to because you demonstrated the confidence you had in yourself to make yourself vulnerable. It is not an easy thing to reveal where you stand on an issue, share your stated belief on a topic, or to share more about yourself beneath the surface of what others may already know about you personally or professionally. In fact, the majority of people do not like to share information about themselves, especially at work or in professional environments.

For example, while you may have many discussions with someone about a presidential election, you may not reveal if you are a Republican or a Democrat, a member of a Socialist Party or an anti-government regime. Subsequently, you may speak to someone about a natural disaster but not reveal how much you donated to the relief cause, if you made a donation at all, or if you knew someone who was affected by the event. The point is, emotional connections are not always easy, comfortable, or natural in the context of a conversation or networking opportunity. When used well, however, they will help you master the art of connection. So here are some tips on how to effectively use emotional connections as a way to connect with others.

Family First

For the most part, people like to talk about their family, pets, kids, homes, or other familial things associated with their life outside the context of their professional environment. So ask them about it! The quicker you get someone to begin sharing more around this dimension the easier it will be for you to establish a connection. Be prepared, however, to share details about your family environment in a similar context so you can level the playing field as part of the conversation.

Stay (K)urrent

Current events or happenings, those that make the national news headlines each day, typically evoke strong opinions. From the celebrity gossip column to a story about a product recall to news about a major crime conspiracy theory, current events are a great way to connect with someone in the context of a conversation. So prepare to make a connection by always having five topics from the current day's news that you will bring up in the context of a conversation or when networking with colleagues.

Storytelling

When speaking to someone on a topic, the experience of a friend, colleague, or someone you heard about can be just as valuable in helping you to establish a connection with others. Conversations are in many ways a collection of stories drawn from current or past experiences. Have a set of topics and a set of stories that you can share about people's experiences that help you relate to people in various ways.

For example, based on the event or setting, I try to have three topics that I am comfortable sharing with others centered around my family, my prior professional experiences, and my motivations in life. I accompany these topics with stories of other people who may have shared a similar path or family experiences to help illustrate points I make in a conversation.

The more you are able to connect through sharing stories, the more you help the person who you are speaking with relate to a topic or issue that may be of concern. This helps establish a closer connection to that person. In essence, by sharing stories, you are performing a service to help others relate to the context or content of the conversation.

Listen With Your Mouth Closed

We often underestimate the value of listening. When we listen, we allow others to share, and by doing so we create a natural bond with the person sharing. Listening with your mouth closed can be a hard thing to do, especially when you have a response or opinion to what is being shared. When you are able to listen with an open mind and closed mouth, you send a signal that you care about what is being said. This signal is then translated to a closer connection you establish just because you honored the nonverbal contract of waiting before speaking.

If this is something that is hard for you to do in the context of a conversation, try using the praying hands stance in front of your mouth while listening to the other person speak. This will convey that you are thinking, listening, and help you keep your mouth shut so you can effectively stay in tune with the conversation and the emotional lift that you are providing by listening.

Deflect and Uplift

When you can uplift someone you build an automatic emotional connection. This can happen both consciously and unconsciously in the context of a conversation. For example, when someone says to you, "what a horrible day," you have two choices. You may either agree and set the tone of the conversation with a negative thought, or you can deflect the statement and turn the tone of the conversation back to a positive orientation by saying, "Actually it's going to be a great day."

Your ability to what I call "deflect and uplift" can help you establish strong connections with others and help shape positive attributes associated with your personal brand. I have found that people appreciate a little positive inspiration in the normal context of a conversation. I also make a point to try to deflect negative conversation starters as a way to maintain a focus on creating a positive connection.

The next time someone starts a conversation with you and begins with a negative theme try to deflect it by turning it around to a more positive topic. They will appreciate you for it and you will establish a greater connection as a result.

Emotional connections build lasting connections and strengthen the perception others take away from a conversation with you.

Verbal Connection

People make an immediate connection based on the tone of voice and enthusiasm of their greeting. However, we often do not pay attention to our voice in conversation, and may not be maximizing our full potential in establishing a connection with others.

Have you ever noticed the tone of your voice when you greet someone? The next time you greet someone, notice the tone of your voice and how much enthusiasm you put into your "hello."

If you analyze and break down what I call your "greeting tones," the people you are most closest too, or get the most enjoyment from being around, usually get the most enthusiastic greeting. These are also the people with whom you establish the strongest connections. It's our equivalent to assigning someone a ringtone on our cellular phone. On the flip side, the people we are less concerned about, those with whom we are less interested in getting to know, typically get a greeting with a lower voice tone and less enthusiasm. These are the people with whom we develop weaker connections and often try to avoid.

Intuitively, it is obvious to come to this conclusion. People react differently to people who they want to establish a connection with, and thus our voice inflection reveals our level of interest. A 1997 *Psychology Today* article titled "A Different Tone of Voice," by Anne Murphy Paul, noted that lullabies strengthen the emotional ties between a parent and their child.[10]

Similarly, a conversation is like a lullaby. When you are able to create a lullaby in your conversation, it will strengthen the connection you have with others. So here are some tips on mastering the art of verbal connection.

Turn Your Volume to High, Medium, or Low

Before you greet someone, take two-tenths of a second to make a decision about your greeting volume. Based on the type of connection you want to establish with someone, make a determination on how you will set your volume. We often don't pay attention to this detail when meeting others, but it is an important one when trying to make a connection. If it is someone you know well, like a lot, or are particularly interested in speaking with, turn your greeting volume to high.

A high note greeting is characterized by an inflection in your voice that conveys an expectation of pleasure from the ensuing conversation. It is a great tool to establish a connection with someone in a position of power, authority, or celebrity status, especially when used to demonstrate flattery or appreciation of one's accomplishments. Be careful, however, not to overuse or misuse your high volume setting as it can also give off a negative impression that you are overly anxious, prematurely comfortable, or trying too hard to make an impression.

A medium greeting volume is characterized by little to no inflection in your voice when greeting someone. It is best used in a formal setting or instance when you are trying to make a more serious impression or you are unsure of the level of connection the other person wants to establish with you. A good use of the medium greeting volume is for a job interview where you want to focus one's initial perceptions on your skills and build a gradual impression on your personality over time.

The low greeting tone is characterized by a deliberate voice inflection below the level of your regular speaking voice. It is best used when you are trying to discretely convey a lack of interest in connecting with the person you are speaking with, to convey strength or dominance, or to convey some other concern, dissonance, or barrier to making a connection. For example, if you meet someone who you have heard negative things about, you may have a low greeting tone when meeting that person. This conveys your hesitation in establishing a connection or having a deeper level of dialogue and may signal that a connection will not be made or is not possible. Conversations that begin with a low greeting tone are much shorter in length than those that begin with a high volume. Going back to the physical connection dimension we explored earlier, you can correlate a high volume greeting with a hug, a medium voice greeting with a firm handshake, and a low voice greeting with a limp handshake. Each combination will have a dramatic impact on how you are able to connect with others.

Gotta Have Rhythm

In addition to your greeting tone, the rhythm of your conversation is an important element in establishing a solid connection with others. Thus it is important to know in advance what type of rhythm you want to have with the person you are speaking with. I define conversation rhythm as the tone of how you enter, how long you stay, and how you get out or leave a conversation with another person.

Conversation rhythm is not something most people think about, because most people let conversations happen. As a result, the rhythm of the conversation plays out by chance. Think about the conversations you have with others. How conscious are you of your rhythm?

You may not be aware of your conversation rhythm when you are speaking or networking. However, when you understand the rhythm of conversations, you can dramatically improve your ability to establish meaningful connections and favorable impressions with others. Conversations typically take on a variety of rhythm patterns. For example:

a. High-Med-High
b. High-Med-Low
c. High-Low-High
d. Low-Med-High
e. Med-Med-High
f. Med-High-Med
g. Low-Low-Low

These are examples of rhythm tone patterns that occur from conversations you have every day. For example, sometimes you may greet someone with a high tone, and because of something that is revealed in the conversation, you end or leave the conversation on a low note. Other times you may start a conversation with a low greeting and end up on a "high note."

Ideally you want to enter with a high greeting tone. This conveys interest in establishing a connection. You want to maintain the conversation with a medium voice tone and energy and then leave the conversation on a high note with an inflection in your voice that conveys you were thankful for the experience of having a conversation and look forward to counting that person as one of your contacts.

We often throw around the term "end on a high note" and use it to describe something that happened to us or the result we want to achieve when retiring or leaving a situation. But this phrase plays an important role in how we connect with others. It has also transcended society, having an impact in sports, politics, performing arts, and business.

The phrase actually got its roots from the performing arts, specifically, singing. It is a physical challenge to reach ("hit") the highest note in your range, and composers will save the emotional peak of a song or aria for that note. When it is reached, it leaves the audience breathtakingly speechless and is a powerful way to end a performance. When missed, however, it leads to disappointment and can destroy an otherwise flawless performance in one note.

In one memorable broadcast of the Metropolitan Opera, Lily Pons had asked the orchestra to play her final aria a note higher than written, to show off her high C. Alas, Lily Pons and her voice had both grown older, and she hit B-flat instead. It wasn't just a wrong note, it was a note that made the chord into a dominant-seventh, a harsh sounding chord that transposed the key and left everyone hanging on a half-cadence. It was an embarrassment for the singer and production.

The point is, how you begin, maintain, and leave a conversation will have an impact on the type of connection you make with others. For example, I always try to enter a conversation on a high rhythm tone, using a high volume greeting or medium, as appropriate. I then carry on the conversation with a medium voice tone and medium rhythm, meaning I maintain the same level of voice inflection. And finally, I try to leave or close the conversation on a high by thanking the person for the meeting or conversation, setting up a next time to chat, and leaving them with a reminder of something positive we both established during the conversation.

As you begin to focus and become more conscious of your conversation rhythm, you will find the rhythm tone that works best for you, acknowledging that it will change depending on the person you are speaking with or meeting.

Do note that when you start a conversation with a low rhythm tone of voice you will have an uphill battle during the conversation to end on a high note. As a result you may be more challenged in establishing solid connections with others.

Experience Connection

The fifth and final dimension of connection is the experience connection. The experience connection is one of the strongest dimensions for making yourself memorable or what I call "brand recall" coming out of a conversation.

According to David Middleton and Steve Brown, authors of *The Social Psychology of Experience*, the connection between what we have lived and our memory has a direct impact on social interaction. The authors reveal that memories do not solely reside in a linear passage of time, linking past, present and future, nor do they solely rest within the individual's consciousness, but that memory sits at the very heart of "lived experience." Whether collective or individual, the vehicle for how we remember or forget is linked to social interaction, object interaction, and the different durations of living that we all have. It is very much connected to the social psychology of experience.

Another way to look at this is what we live we remember. As it relates to establishing a connection with others, what we share about what we live is what others ultimately remember. Think about the examples or life experiences you may have shared in your conversation. More than likely, the more dramatic and vivid the experiences, the more memorable you became as a result. To master the art of connection, find a way to weave in a personal story or image of an experience that is unique to you or shared among you and the person you are speaking with.

Experiences will make you memorable and give you permission to establish a deeper connection with others. So create a game plan by having a preset list of personal experiences across a variety of categories that you are able to share at any trigger point in a conversation. For example, people often make quick associations along several categories:

- Location of inhabitance or birthplace
- Rank or association with power or authority
- Time
- Life experiences
- Travel
- National or ethnic background
- Sports affiliation
- Food preferences
- Weather

Do you have a personal experience or story to correspond to each of these categories that you can share in a conversation with anyone at anytime? If your answer is no, then I encourage you to do this next exercise.

Take some time to reflect and write out examples of personal experiences that you can use later in any conversation. What may seem like a tedious exercise will actually help you to become a better conversationalist and drive more meaningful connections with others. By completing the lines below you will prepare yourself to master the art of connection.

Location of inhabitance or birthplace

Write a unique personal experience about your birthplace, birth circumstances, or where you currently reside.

____

____

____

____

Rank or association with power or authority

Write a unique personal experience about your grade, employment status, current job or career level, or any experiences that stand out with your superiors or authority figures.

____

____

____

____

Time

Write a unique personal experience about your birthday, how you manage time, used time wisely or poorly, benefited from having time on your side, or your overall philosophy on time and aging.

____

____

____

____

Life experiences

Write a unique personal experience about a particular event or experience that changed your life.

____

____

____

____

Travel

Write a unique personal experience about a place you traveled to or remember vividly or a place you always wanted to visit.

____

____

____

____

National or ethnic background

Write a unique personal experience about your national or ethnic background that others may not know or an interesting fact about your heritage.

____

____

____

____

Sports affiliation

Write a unique personal experience about you and sports. For example, your favorite sports team, a team you dislike, a sport you like to watch, or a sport where you attended a game live at a stadium or arena.

____

____

____

____

Food preferences

Write a unique personal experience about you and food. For example, your favorite food, favorite restaurant, an interesting meal that you had in another country, or a food fact that most others would not know.

____

____

____

____

The weather

Write a unique personal experience about you and the weather. For example, have you ever experienced a tornado? What is your favorite season? Have you ever been in a weather emergency or natural disaster?

____

____

____

____

Each of these categories are common conversation topics in a formal business networking situation or casual conversation environment. As you begin to build your inventory of personal experiences across each of the categories, you will be able to proactively select certain experiences that you can bring up in a conversation to help you become more memorable. This is one of the first steps to personal brand planning and as you do so you will achieve meaningful, purpose-filled connections with those you encounter.

How to Become a Connector

An effective way to master the art of connection is to become what I call a "connector." A connector is someone who may not be the most important person in a room, but is the most valuable at that present moment because they are able to connect people of like stature and interests to other people of like stature and interests. People who are deemed connectors usually know a lot of people and have a wide extensive network. As a result, they are able to know and represent the interests of many and are among the first to see when a connection can be made between the like interests of one party to another. To become a connector you must have a sense of the value that one party can bring to another. In other words, you must be able to look at people as products that meet services.

In networking situations, I often make it a point to connect at least one person to another person of like interest. By doing so, I not only get to establish another connection, but I begin to create the notion that I can add value through my knowledge of who should know whom. As a connector you will also be invited to many more opportunities where you can demonstrate your personal brand based on the reputation you establish for connecting others to opportunity.

So how do you become a connector and begin to drive even more meaningful connections with those you encounter. Here are some tips.

Agent 99

When you meet people, especially in networking situations, how often do you ask them what they are looking to achieve from the networking event? Have you ever asked someone who they are looking to meet? Most people do not ask because they are focused on making their own connections and seeking opportunistic moments to have a conversation with someone of importance or influence.

To be a connector, you must willingly take on the role of someone's agent during an event. This is not a role most people will ask you to take on their behalf, nor will they deliberately select you as their representative. As an agent, however, you will create value by delivering the unexpected connection or making the unplanned introduction of one person to another. This is how opportunity can be created, and when relationships blossom as a result of the connections you manufactured for someone else, your personal brand value will increase. You will be memorable forever.

E-mail Introductions

A connector does not limit his or her work to a live meeting room setting. You can be an effective connector behind the scenes after hours. When you return from a networking event, if you were able to work the room you will now have a stack of cards that you will act upon, file for later use, or allow to collect dust over time.

Like effective networkers, effective connectors follow up on all business cards received after an event by sending e-mails to the contacts they made. A connector, however, takes this process one step further by using the e-mail follow-up to recommend an additional contact or service to the person they recently met. By doing this, you show that you actively listened to the conversation and you provide a service contact to help the person you met connect to others who can advance their respective interests.

An e-mail introduction from a connector is a great way to establish connections with others, especially because it comes with a built-in endorsement. As a connector you are indirectly giving an endorsement of one person to another, which makes you a broker of connection. When a match strikes, you will be the one that all roads lead back to, which allows you to establish a meaningful connection with both parties.

So the next time you send a follow-up e-mail after meeting someone, see if you can double the value of your follow-up by connecting them to another one of your contacts. This strategy will help you become a better connector and build a positive association for your personal brand at the same time.

Conclusion

The topics shared in this chapter are designed to make you think about your normal interactions with others and how to transform them to become extraordinary encounters. Your connectability will increase your appeal as a personal brand and your confidence in situations where making connections are critical to personal and professional success. As you begin to incorporate these tactics, you will become more aware of how you communicate verbally and nonverbally, the topics you bring up in a conversation, and effective ways to help others by being a connector. All will put you well on your way to mastering the art of connection.

The more you can connect with someone, the more likely you will become and leave a memorable impression.

Chapter 8K

Know That Silence is Not an Option

In This Chapter

- Making yourself memorable
- Reducing absence of mention
- Tooting your own horn
- Having a meeting strategy
- Using the Internet to brand yourself

Personal branding is a proactive behavior that influences your ability to be sought after, mentioned, valued, and given a second, third, and fourth look. People remember brands that are memorable. Memorable brands loudly appeal to customers through a variety of channels and touchpoints including advertising, visual identity, packaging, and product design. Silent brands are those we don't recall, don't remember, don't use, and therefore don't value.

According to marketing guru and author Peter Fisk, a good brand can account for fifty percent of a company's market value. I would take this a step further and say that a good brand whose value is not known is not a good brand, is fifty percent less memorable than leading brands, and has a fifty percent greater chance of becoming extinct.

To be silent is to be undiscovered, and when you are undiscovered your brand value diminishes over time. In this chapter we will explore strategies to establish recall so that your personal brand never goes undiscovered and you can create an overarching voice that accentuates your uniqueness.

Reducing Absence of Mention

Merriam-Webster dictionary defines silence as **1:** forbearance from speech or noise **:** muteness —often used interjectionally**2:** absence of sound or noise **:** stillness <in the *silence* of the night>**3:** absence of mention.

To build an effective personal brand, you want to eliminate the absence of mention of your brand when it comes to things you have a specific capability or competency for delivering. In other words you want to be in what many call "the considered set."

The considered set is the first set of variables that come to mind when you say or hear a particular subject matter. When you are in the considered set you are creating a memorable impression that allows you to be top of mind. When you are top of mind it is you and your personal brand that gets picked first, selected out of many, referred with an endorsement, rated number one, and becomes best in class. You don't get there, however, by being silent. So another way to think about this is: "Good products leave memorable impressions and good people leave memorable impressions."

Total Recall

To illustrate this point, let's do a quick exercise. It's an exercise I call "total recall." Let's see how it works for you.

Write the first brand name that comes to mind when you see the words below.

1. Coffee ____________________
2. French fries ____________________
3. Watches ____________________
4. Soda ____________________
5. Running sneakers ____________________
6. Electronics ____________________
7. Computers ____________________
8. Discount shopping ____________________
9. Luxury hotels ____________________
10. Leather ____________________

While I am not there to see your responses, let's see if I can read your mind. I'll bet the answers to one through ten begin and end with the following letters.

1.	S-------s	6.	S--y
2.	M-------s	7.	D----l or A---e
3.	R---x	8.	W-----t or T----t
4.	C--e or P---i	9.	R--z C-----n
5.	N--e	10.	C---h or W-----s

How did I do? Did I read your mind? I am going to guess that I got somewhere between eight of ten or nine out of ten correct Typically when I conduct this exercise to live audiences I score between nine out of ten and ten out of ten correct responses. So here's another way to think about it. If you are silent, you are leaving it up to others to give you a "brand." And, in many cases the brand they give you is "none at all." What I call, "the brand of no recall." Now let's go back to that recall exercise you did above. I have inserted the answer key here so you can check your responses against mine.

(Answer key: 1. Starbucks 2. McDonald's 3. Rolex 4. Coke or Pepsi 5. Nike 6. Sony 7. Dell or Apple 8. Wal-Mart or Target 9. Ritz Carlton 10. Coach or Wilson's)

The product names you did not mention are the ones in many cases you could not recall or the ones you did not think were "good." For example, for "french fries" you did not write the corner deli on 86th street, rather I guessed that you would write McDonalds. For "electronics" you did not write E-Z Tech Electronics rather, I guessed that you would write Sony. So if "good products leave memorable impressions" and "good people leave memorable impressions" then if people cannot "commit you to recall," chances are they may also not think you are good.

So here are some tips for making yourself memorable.

Make Your Personal Appearance Appear

In chapter 7K I explored the importance of knowing what your personal appearance says about you before you enter a room. To make your self memorable, you must proactively appear with a distinct personal appearance that allows you to stand out and to be noticed.

If you think about the brands you are able to look for in a specific category, because you are aware of their packaging, you know exactly what to look for and what to expect. As a result, your recall of the product is high. Similarly, when you create a distinct identifier in your personal appearance people will know what to look for when they see you, what to expect when they see you, and therefore you will achieve a high level of recall with those you encounter.

Put Your Brand Into Action

Brands that perform well are remembered for their performance and thus achieve first mention in their category. For example, instead of saying "pass the tissue" today many people say "pass the Kleenex." Kleenex the brand has become synonymous with the category of tissue because of its performance. A focus on performance will allow you to be well-known in a category and thus be remembered for specific behaviors and actions that can be attributed to your personal brand.

To become a memorable brand, identify a specific skill, action, achievement, behavior or capability that you exude that is unique and can always be traced back to you. For example, as a saxophone player I am often introduced as the guy who plays the saxophone. This is a skill that I have developed that I demonstrate often when I am in public settings. As a result, others are able to recall this attribute as a part of my personal brand and are then able to recall my name. I am not saying that you have to go out and now learn how to play the tuba, but find or pick a skill that is unique to you that you can demonstrate in public settings to begin to drive recall of your brand.

Be a Lifeline

Think about the brands that provide a remedy for an illness or a quick fix to a problem. These are brands we readily recall and remember based on what they do to help or fix a situation. For example, when you want to get rid of insects you may run out and get a can of Raid. When you have a cold you may rely on NyQuil. And when you have a cut you may reach for a Band-Aid. The point I am making is that people remember product brands that address or help fix a problem or issue. When you help others, uplift others, bring others along, mentor others, refer others, or simply listen to others to help them cope, you develop a brand for being helpful. People remember people that help others.

So to become a memorable personal brand, get in touch with the ways that you help others. Become a remedy to an issue, a problem solver, a fix-it person, a soothing relief, an inspiring vote of confidence, a coach, a supportive friend. Whatever it is, become someone who helps others. This will allow you to achieve a greater level of recall with those you encounter and those who tell others of the great help that you are.

Toot Your Horn

The brands we remember are the ones whose advertising campaigns, marketing slogans, logos, reviews, and public relations activities are the loudest and most consistently in our face. We often struggle with tooting our own horn. It is something that many struggle with today because of the uncomfortable nature of promoting ourselves.

The *Psychology Today* article, "Success in the Land of the Less," by S.J. Liu and A.E. Katz, says that in the process of promoting ourselves, we often confuse acceptance with self-respect. We want so badly for everyone to like us that we may neglect those who love us the most and make it almost impossible to love ourselves. Then, when outsiders don't buy our promotional package, we feel that we've failed.

All too often the concentration on a packaged image also eclipses the development of the skill, talent, and creativity that are required for real growth and advancement. As a result, the self-promoter can end up losing both psychologically and professionally when the employer or buyers begin to look for the substance inside that impressive package.

When it comes to promoting yourself, you may be your worst enemy and your harshest critic. While it may not be comfortable to tell others what you do, how well you do it, and what others have said about how you have helped them, it is vital to being a memorable brand. It is not enough to rely on your skill and talent alone to get you further ahead in life and your career. You must toot your own horn, and toot it loud enough so that others can hear your tune, and share your music with a friend.

When I learned how to play the saxophone, I also learned how to metaphorically toot my own horn. As a musician, every note I play is played to be heard by someone else. When I improvise or come up with a vibrant jazz solo, I am communicating with the audience and telling them a story of music, life, or whatever mood I was in at the time. Tooting your own horn as it relates to telling others of your accomplishments is very similar to telling a story. In fact, if you think about it as telling a story versus telling someone how great you are, you may have an easier time with tooting your own horn.

The details are really in the delivery. Here are some tips to make you more comfortable tooting your own horn.

1. **"You" are the "I" in "we":** When sending e-mails or letters letting others know what a great job you did, replace the uses of "I" with "we." As you do, you will be more comfortable giving exact details of the wonderful things that you have accomplished. And, while you may be attributing the outcome to the collective team, by virtue of you being the author of the correspondence, you will be the one that others attribute the great things you mentioned in your message. In essence, in your promotion the "I" becomes "we," but in the evaluation and credit given for the effort, the "we" becomes "you."
2. **Make a mission to your brand ambassadors**: As I mentioned in chapter 5K, a great way to promote yourself is through your brand ambassadors. Brand ambassadors are those people who have access to the persons of influence you want to reach. They are accessible and share the great things you have accomplished with people of influence without your knowing. If you have done something great, something worth talking about, but you don't want to come right out and say "I'm great" for fear of being perceived as too self-absorbed, find the people who can get the message of your accomplishment to the ear of the right people. You will be tooting your own horn in the process but will be playing with a friendly band.
3. **Start a therapy practice**: One of the best and most effective strategies to promote yourself is to offer and ask for advice. When you offer or ask for advice based on something you have already accomplished, you will strike the balance between helping someone and letting them know what you accomplished. As you do this you will grant others permission to hear all the wonderful things that you have done and at the same time gain permission to share them with others. This is a subtle but effective way to toot your horn. Here's an example to illustrate this point. You may start a conversation or correspondence by saying, "I see that we have a problem with 'abc' situation. I was thinking how I could help or be of assistance. I would like your advice on this suggestion."

By following this approach you have created a safe environment to share your accomplishments in a manner that promotes yourself and is positioned as offering a suggestion and asking for advice. When you ask for advice in this context, you are simply asking for someone to pay attention to your accomplishments.

Tooting your own horn is not easy, but with a crafty approach to getting yourself heard and noticed, you will achieve great recall for your personal brand.

Have a Meeting Strategy

Have you ever been in a meeting or left a discussion and asked "Why is that person here? What did they contribute to the discussion?" Have you ever come upon a great idea only to have someone think of it in a different way, and what I call, "beat you to your own punch line?" These are the times when silence can count against you and diminish the value of your personal brand.

A meeting is an opportunity to be heard and a venue for your personal brand to be on display. Many people, however, walk in and out of meetings without saying a word, and thus become invisible. When people don't see you, hear you, or know you are present, it is hard for them to believe you actually add value. So to become memorable and to increase the value of your personal brand when attending a meeting it is important to have a meeting strategy.

Step One: Decide what role you will play before the meeting begins. On average there are ten roles that people play at a meeting.

1. **The Facilitator**: This is the person who sets up the meeting or call, invites the attendees, walks the group through the agenda, opens the meeting with introductory remarks, closes the meeting, and outlines the next steps and course of actions
2. **The Stenographer**: This person usually works closely with the facilitator and has the sole responsibility for taking notes. They record the points made, actions suggested, attendees present, tasks assigned, and provide a complete account of the meeting event to be filed in the archive files for future retrieval.
3. **The Connector**: This person may not share much in the way of original thought but plays a vital role in connecting points made between parties so that the group can keep focused on consensus. The connector is sometimes criticized for "stealing ideas" or "repackaging someone else's thoughts," but the value they bring in finding like elements between points helps the meeting move along and therefore they are able to withstand the criticism that comes from this role.
4. **The Devil's Advocate**: This person, also known as "the contrarian" is the person most people in the meeting love to hate. The devil's advocate always has an opposing view as a counterargument to

what is being proposed. This person gives in to consensus only as a last resort or if their point of view has been accepted. Devil's advocates play a critical role in that they keep the group honest and open to seeing the consequences of actions proposed or to see another viewpoint that may alter the recommendation of the group. It takes courage or rank to maintain the devil's advocate role, but those who are good at this usually are the most vocal, most memorable, and most valuable attendee in the meeting.

5. **The Loud Listener**: This person is one of the quietest people in the meeting. They usually do not speak more than four times, however each time they speak they direct the verbal meeting traffic in a positive direction. Loud listeners take in the meeting; they listen, ponder, analyze, internalize, and wait for when there is verbal gridlock. Like a traffic cop, it is at this moment that they insert their authority, grab the group's attention and refocus the group in a positive direction. A loud listener is a very valuable person to have in a meeting, and although they do not say much, they are very valuable to helping the meeting achieve its end goal and resolution.
6. **The Private Investigator**: This person is usually invited to the meeting as an optional attendee or finds a way to invite him or herself. The private investigator usually works for someone who cannot attend the meeting but will be impacted by the outcome or result of actions agreed upon by the attendees. The PI's job is to "report back." This person will typically not say much, but will pay special attention and observe body language. Their job is to give an account of the crime scene and to build a case against one or all of the attendees at the meeting. You can usually spot a PI because they voluntarily sit in the back of the room or furthest away from the facilitator. The PI scouts for facts and clues that could indicate a pending assignment or action that could be unfavorable to the party he or she is representing.
7. **The Reporter**: This person's job is to report news or information valuable to the broader discussion. At times the reporter is the one who dominates the meeting airtime because they have the most information and up-to-date data on the subject matter being discussed. Reporters love data and use data as a way to make themselves valuable. The more data they can share, the more airtime they will have, which often translates into the more value from their attendance at the meeting.
8. **The Victim**: This person or their respective department is most often the subject or reason for the meeting. From the start of the

meeting to the end they are put on trial and subject to interrogation by the meeting attendees. The victim's primary role is to state their case and convince the attendees that they are innocent or seek remediation if they are guilty. Primary examples of victims are those who enter a meeting to plead their case for funding. They are subject to questioning, fear tactics, and sometimes have to call on witnesses to help substantiate their position. The victim is not the most desirable role in a meeting, it is not a role that most choose to assume but sometimes this role cannot be avoided. One tip, though. Everyone remembers the victim.

9. **The Student**: This person is invited to the meeting as a developmental exercise. The student has no legitimate role or accountability for anything that takes place at the meeting. They have been invited to be exposed to the subject matter which will help prepare the student for challenges ahead.
10. **The Question Mark**: This is the person you don't want to be. This person attends the meeting but does not say a word, leaves the meeting without speaking to anyone, and is generally a mystery to the other attendees as to how and why they were invited to attend. Question marks usually do not speak up because of fear, lack of self-esteem, or lack of knowledge of the subject matter being discussed. They will often try to get on the good side of the stenographer so they can get the notes in lieu of being vocal in the meeting. Unfortunately, many people become question marks in a meeting without knowing it and therefore their personal brand suffers as a result. The feedback on most question marks is that they do not add any value.

So there you have it, the ten roles of a meeting. To become a memorable personal brand, you must avoid silence at all times. As you review these ten meeting roles, it is important to decide and communicate in advance the role that you will play in a meeting or venue where your personal brand will be on display. By analyzing these meeting roles, you should now never walk into a meeting without thinking about the role that you will play.

As you become more aware of these roles, begin to think about which ones you play most often, which roles you seek to pattern yourself after, and which ones you want to avoid at all cost. Having a meeting strategy will help you to avoid being silent. As you become less silent you become more confident, which raises your ability to deliver more value. As with great brands, people remember the brands that deliver the greatest value.

Size Eight Please

When you go into a store and try on an article of clothing are you more likely to buy the product? If you sit in the driver's seat of a car and test drive it to experience how it drives are you more likely to buy the car? If you eat a free sample of a food product and taste its flavor are you more likely to make a purchase? The answer to all of these questions is YES!!! Great brands become memorable brands because consumers try them first before they buy. Research shows that trial leads to recall which leads to eventual purchase.

Consumer package goods companies, like Procter & Gamble and Unilever have used this technique for decades by mailing free samples of laundry detergent and shampoo to homes. A January 2001 survey by the Brand Marketing and the Promotion Marketing Association found that sampling is highly effective for marketers of consumer packaged goods. It asked 1,195 people about their free sample habits. The results:

1. Ninety-five percent have tried a sample
2. Thirty-eight percent have tried every sample they received in the past year
3. Ninety-two percent decided to buy a grocery, household, or health and beauty care product after trying a sample
4. Seventy-three percent became aware of new or improved products through samples
5. Eighty-four percent would consider switching products if they liked the free sample

Many consumer software companies let prospective customers try a product for a limited time. Customers download a full-featured version of the software from the company's Web site for free before it expires after thirty to ninety days, or a limited number of uses. Other companies have taken similar measures to induce trial.

- Krispy Kreme: New customers who have yet to try a Krispy Kreme doughnut are often handed one in the store. Sometimes clerks include an extra doughnut to munch on while waiting to pay.
- SolutionPeople: This creativity consulting firm for the Fortune 500 charges sixty to one hundred thousand dollars for several days of creative brainstorming. Prospective customers can send a representative to a day-long public session for eight hundred fifty dollars. The company reports a conversion rate of more than two-thirds to the more expensive service offering.

Customers can also purchase a handheld tool that encapsulates the company's creative process for seventy-five dollars.

- Dallas Mavericks: What's it like to be a season-ticket holder for this NBA team? Fans can find out by buying five and ten game packets of tickets. If customers like their seats and the overall experience, they can upgrade to a half or full-season membership. The team's marketing chief says fifty-five percent of customers upgrade.
- IBM: Its "Test Drive" program lets programmers test Linux applications online in a simulated IBM environment without having to actually buy IBM hardware.
- Salesforce.com: This fast-growing software company offers Web-based sales force automation and customer relationship management tools. To establish itself in the market, it offered customers free use of tools for one year.

The point I am making is that to make yourself memorable, you must give others access to try you on, take you for a test drive, research your benefits, and experience the results of your performance. When people experience you they remember you. Big companies know this. They understand that if the brand is memorable customers are more likely to want to be affiliated with the product and thus will make a purchase. You should know this too as it relates to your personal brand. Here are some tips, using the Internet and other channels, on how to give people access to you so you can become a memorable brand.

Business Cards—Don't Leave Home Without Them

Your business card is a ticket to opportunity. Have business cards with you at all times, even in the oddest of places. You never know where the opportunity for you to become memorable to someone else will present itself. I make a point to carry business cards with me wherever I go just to be ready for that unexpected encounter that could lead to opportunity.

I once met a professional contact while sitting on a bus of all places. Both of us did not know at the time that we would eventually end up working at the same company, and years later attending each other's weddings, but that's how life happens when you are prepared to make yourself memorable. Because I was armed with my business cards I was able to establish a connection and provide a way for my contact to reach me, which tipped off a great friendship—one which we continue to maintain today.

Your business cards should convey your personal brand and naturally be an extension of the service you deliver and the experience that you will provide others when they encounter you.

Build a Google Trail and They Will Follow

Today people use Google to check facts and conduct home background checks on just about everything. Google yourself and see what comes up. If you do not have a Google trail of positive facts about you that support your personal brand, you are not providing others the full access that they are looking for to create an impression of your value. As a result you may be dismissed as a brand not worth having.

The Internet is a vault that holds the permanent record of your personal brand. Begin to use the Internet more as a way to virally give others access to experience you, read up on your accomplishments, and come to a decision as to why they should choose you as the product they buy into. Once you start to build your online brand remember that your online personal brand will become your offline brand and it will be hard to separate the two.

As many online enthusiasts have cited, your brand cannot hide from Google. So give Google the right things to say about you so you can become the most memorable brand on planet Internet.

Why Not Wiki

A wiki is a collection of Web pages designed to enable anyone who accesses it to contribute or modify content, using a simplified markup language. Wikis are often used to create collaborative Web sites and to power community Web sites. They are becoming great tools to transform yourself, your product, and your personal brand into an encyclopedia of memorable facts.

Social Media is the ATM for Your Personal Brand

With social media, the more personal brand currency you deposit, the more recall you can withdraw later for your brand. Authoring a public online journal, more commonly known as blogging, has become a worldwide personal branding phenomenon. In addition, there are great Web sites today that allow you to become a well-known celebrity on the Internet by tapping into communities of people who share common interests, a thirst for knowledge, and want to find cool stuff.

Making yourself memorable on the Internet means being the "cool stuff" people are looking for and finding the widest and most interested audience to share it with. So here are ten Web sites that will allow you to gain maximum exposure. Of course there are hundreds more so I will leave you discover them on your own.

Digg (www.digg.com)
Digg is a place for people to discover and share content across the web, from the biggest online destinations to the most obscure blog. Digg surfaces the best stuff as voted on by the site's own registered community of users.

FaceBook (www.facebook.com)
Facebook is a social utility that connects people with friends and others who work, study, and live around them. People use Facebook to keep up with friends, upload an unlimited number of photos, share links and videos, and learn more about the people they meet.

StumbleUpon (www.stumbleupon.com)
StumbleUpon helps you discover and share great Web sites. As you click or Stumble!, the site delivers high-quality pages matched to your personal preferences. These pages have been explicitly recommended by your friends or one of over five million other websurfers with interests similar to you. The site gives you a chance to rate the sites you like ( ) and automatically shares them with like-minded people—and helps you discover great sites your friends recommend.

Flickr (www.flickr.com)
Flickr is one of the best online photo management and sharing applications in the world. The site's primary objectives are to help people make their content available to the people who have an interest in their content and to enable new ways to arrange and organize videos and pictures.

Twitter (www.twitter.com)
Twitter is a service for friends, family, and co-workers to communicate and stay connected through the exchange of quick, frequent answers to one simple question: **What are you doing?**

FeedBurner (www.feedburner.com)
FeedBurner is the leading provider of media distribution and audience engagement services for blogs and RSS feeds. The site's Web-based tools help bloggers, podcasters, and commercial publishers promote, deliver and profit from their content on the Web.

Wetpaint (www.wetpaint.com)
A Wetpaint Web site is built on the power of collaborative thinking. The site allows you to create Web sites that mix all the best features of wikis, blogs, forums, and social networks into a rich, user-generated community based around whatever content you desire to feature.

YouTube (www.youtube.com)
YouTube is the leader in online video, and the premier destination to watch and share original videos worldwide through a Web experience. YouTube allows people to easily upload and share video clips on www.youtube.com and across the Internet through Web sites, mobile devices, blogs, and e-mail.

Reddit (www.reddit.com)
Reddit is a source for what's new and popular online. The site allows users to vote on links that you like or dislike and help decide what's popular, or submit your own site for review!

Del.icio.us (http://del.icio.us/)
Del.icio.us is a **social bookmarking** Web site whose primary use is to store your bookmarks online. You can also use del.icio.us to see the interesting links that your friends and other people bookmark, and share links with them in return. You can even browse and search del.icio.us to discover the cool and useful bookmarks that everyone else has saved which is made easy with tags. The site allows you to access the same bookmarks from any computer and add bookmarks from anywhere in the world. The site provides a more flexible system than using folders.

These cool Web sites and useful social media tools will help you become famous overnight. Social Web sites are ideal venues to build your personal brand. They are effective for individuals and groups of people who are connected by a common interest and need to collaborate. Instead of sending e-mails back and forth, a social Web site can be used to centralize the knowledge of a group or community. Because the social Web site can be edited by anyone with the proper permissions, you can keep everyone in your group up-to-date and actively involved. This means more frequent opportunities to make yourself memorable.

Keep Your Door Open

If you sit in an office or enclosed area, chances are people will walk by and look into your working space. It's human nature to stare into an open area or to look into a room with an open door. If you want to be remembered, keep your door open. I liken having an open door to what happens on the Internet with Web sites. As people walk by your space and peer into your open office or location they are essentially clicking onto your "yousite." The more clicks or visits to your location the more impressions you are making and thus the more memorable you have made yourself.

Each day you get many unique visitors, and if they come into your office and stay for a while you will be increasing your session time. Sometimes they call others into your office and thus you are getting links from other sources. Sometimes you'll hear people talking about you right next to your open space; these people are essentially blogging about you. Having an open door will help you build impressions over time that makes you a memorable brand.

Elevator Management

Did you know that you can increase your ability to be memorable by managing what hour of the day you take the elevator? If you work in a building with an elevator, take special notice of the time that you arrive to the elevator lobby each day and who arrives at that time with you. We are often creatures of habit and schedule, especially those who have a morning or evening routine. The more you see the same people who arrive and leave at the same time as you, the more likely you are to become memorable to those persons. This is because you will have built many impressions over time just by frequently being in the same place at the same time. Here's why this can be a powerful tool to establish your brand or make a connection with someone in a high position of leadership authority.

- **6 AM – 7 AM CEO shift:** Have you ever wondered what time a CEO gets to work? According to the US Department of Labor, nearly twenty-nine million employees start their day between 4:30 AM and 7:29 AM. A greater proportion of these employees are CEOs. Many reports indicate that CEOs on average arrive to their offices between 6 AM and 7 AM each day. So if this is the case, then one way to become memorable, and maybe bump into a CEO, is to begin riding the elevators between the hours of 6 AM and 7 AM. You will be surprised at whom you may see entering a building at this hour, but in many cases you have a higher likelihood of running into a CEO or top executive.

- **The significance of 11:45 AM and 2:15 PM:** Your elevator speech is only as good as the opportunity that can be created while you are in that space. For business professionals, many power lunches happen between the hours of 12 noon and 2 PM, with ninety minutes being devoted to conversation and thirty minutes of actual eating time. Because 12 noon and 2 PM are when business is conducted, then 11:45 AM and 2:15 PM represent the time slots where elevators are filled with opportunities to make yourself memorable. Executives looking to get to their 12 noon lunch appointments often leave around 11:45 AM to get to their lunch destination on time and arrive back to the office around 2:15 PM. These time slots are great opportunities to proactively run into people of influence who you can introduce yourself to on an elevator.
- **6 PM to 7 PM:** The hours of 6 PM and 7 PM are great hours to ride the elevator because they give you an opportunity to tell a story or give a recap of your day. When you run into someone who you want to make an impression on in the elevator, these hours provide an excellent opportunity to share a brief end-of-the-day recap. This recap can plant the seed in their minds for what you have accomplished, a problem you solved, or how you helped someone get through a difficult situation. My point is, many senior executives leave their office between 6 PM and 7 PM, if you want to get noticed or have the opportunity to interact with them, your elevator ride during these times may just put you in the way of opportunity.

Trick or Treat

Do you know people who always have candy, chocolate, or a sweet treat at their desk or office location? These are the people who you remember because you have stopped by to go trick or treating. Trick or treating usually leads to conversation and conversation usually leads to recall.

Another way to make yourself memorable is to always have a bowl of sweet treats available for others to come by and take. It's an old office networking technique but highly effective in making yourself known among your colleagues and friends, and is a great way to also become famous. People may not know where to find the fax machine but they will sure know who has the Snickers bars at their desk.

So these are just a few tips to help you establish yourself as a memorable brand with those you encounter. Use them actively as you engage with others and as you plan out the recognition you want to create for your personal brand. Remember that silence is not an option when it comes to effective personal branding.

Personal branding is a proactive behavior that influences your ability to be sought after, mentioned, valued, and given a second, third, and fourth look. People remember brands that are memorable.

Chapter 9K

Know Your Expectations (Not Your Limitations)

In This Chapter

- Managing expectations
- Early labels and your personal brand
- Expectation life cycle
- Effective expectation management strategies
- Overcoming limitations
- The business case for your personal brand

Have you ever thought about what others expect from you? Have you ever been denied an opportunity just because the person granting the opportunity did not expect you to deliver a capability that you know you could exude? This scenario happens all the time and may be limiting you today from achieving your goals. However, when you manage your personal brand, you will be able to manage the expectations that others have of you, thus reducing the likelihood of being passed over for an opportunity.

Managing Expectations

An expectation is defined as the state of looking forward to the coming or occurrence of something. To have an expectation is to anticipate an outcome or consider a result probable or certain. As consumers, we have a set of expectations that we associate with our favorite brands. We expect the shoes we wear to get us to our destination comfortably, the car we drive to be safe, the food we consume to be tasty, and the television we watch to have sound, picture, volume control, and the correct level of brightness. In short, we expect the products we buy to perform in a certain manner, give us an anticipated benefit, and make certain a preconceived result. It is no different with your personal brand.

With an awareness of your personal brand comes an awareness of what others expect from you. At times this can be a stressful thing and put pressure on you to always feel that you have to "perform." However, when you know what others expect from you, this intelligence will help you decode the surveillance equipment that others use to assign you a brand. The ability to decode these messages is a skill that will help you be more conscious of your responses, interactions, and how you represent yourself as "a product," to ensure that you are always delivering on your personal brand value.

Have you ever been in a situation where you were what I call "underexpected"? To be "underexpected" is to not be known or expected to do or achieve something that you know you have the capability to do or achieve. There are many what I call "under-words" that are associated with being underexpected. When you are underexpected you are also undervalued, underestimated, misunderstood, undermined, underrated, and often underpaid. When others underexpect you, they are also telling you that your personal brand does not have the same value that you believe it has. In other words, the extent to which you manage your personal brand will have a direct correlation to what others expect from you.

Early Labels and Your Personal Brand

We have all been underexpected at some point in our lives, and as a consequence may have faced circumstances that were not always the most favorable. For many of us this may have started in our early childhood when we were labeled by one of our parents as "the (fill in the blank) one."

Think back to your childhood or grade school days for a second; what was your label? Were you the smart one, the athletic one, the shy one, the greedy one, the tall one, the pretty one, the fat girl, the one with glasses, the momma's boy, the daddy's girl, the bookworm, the copycat, the crybaby, the princess, the little devil, the cute one, the tattletale, the goody two shoes? Somewhere in this list is a label that you got as a kid and I would bet that you remember your label quite vividly.

For many, this list of labels is further replicated more formally in high school. Here you may have or received labels like "best dressed," "worst dressed," "most likely to succeed," "most likely to drop out," "prom queen," "the jock," "class clown," "most valuable player," "most improved," and "drama queen."

And then for those who went to college you may have continued to accumulate labels and perhaps were known as: "the party animal," "the one in that fraternity or sorority," "the one who lives in that dorm," "the one who is a member of that student association," "the one who hangs out with that crowd," "the biology major."

This cycle of being labeled evolves as you enter the workforce and receive labels like "the one who works in that department," "the creative one," "the analytical one," "the good writer," "the sociable one," "the good team player," "the workaholic," "the one to stay away from," "the one who always gets in early," "the one who gets in late," "the one with no life," "the one everyone talks about."

You have been receiving labels of what others expect from you from the day you were born, and in many cases, the way you internalized those labels has a direct correlation to your personal brand today.

For example, here's my story. Growing up in a family of five siblings I was labeled "the oldest boy." My dad and mom would work the day and night shifts of their respective jobs so there were many days where as kids we were unsupervised between the time my mom left for work and when my dad returned home from his job.

As the oldest boy, I internalized this label to mean that I had the responsibility to take care of my siblings as the "man of the house" when my parents were not home. I also took this expectation to mean that I could not always be outside playing with the rest of kids, but had to make sure the house was in order before my parents returned home. That is what they expected from me as a leader; it was my butt on the line if something went wrong, and so that is what I delivered.

Looking back, that expectation from my parents was replicated in my grade school where I was labeled "the teacher's pet." Then in high school, it continued as I was labeled "the leader," "the varsity team captain," "the student council President," "the student representative on the administrative council." In college, my label became "president of the student league," "co-captain of the freshman track team," "dorm room representative." As I look at my life now working in corporate America, I have held labels like manager, national manager, assistant vice president, senior manager, account supervisor, U.S. leader, and author.

Each of the labels I have worn in life came with an expectation that others had of me based on what they believed I could and would deliver. In any one of the life periods described above, however, had I internalized a different expectation of what others had of me versus what I believed I could deliver, I may have veered toward another course in life. In doing so, I may have missed out on the opportunities that I have gained from being a leader, which was a result of the labels I received in the early years of my life.

But what if you got a bad label early on in your life? Labels like: "the dumb one," "the slow one," "the lazy one," "the fat one," "the skinny one," "the short one," "the retarded one," "the scaredy-cat," "the one who needs special ed," "the one that will never amount to anything," "the bum," "the one who has no friends," "the one with the 'cooties.'" If you were lucky enough to get one of these labels early on in life and you reflect on your life presently, how did that label contribute to the personal brand you live today? Did you internalize it and live to that expectation or did you prove that label wrong?

If you poll many of the great leaders in our world today you'll find there are two commonalities in the labels they were given. They either got a positive label that they lived consistently as a part of building their personal brand, or they got a bad label that they spent their life disproving.

- **Michael Jordan** was cut from his high school basketball team in his sophomore year and later went on to become the world's greatest basketball player.
- **Bill Gates** dropped out of Harvard University and went on to become one of the richest men in the world.
- **NBA basketball legend Julius Erving,** also known as "**Dr. J,**" noted in an interview by the Academy of Achievement that, "**I think I started learning lessons about being a good person long before I ever knew what basketball was. And that starts in the home; it starts with the parental influence. I came from a broken home, so my mom was a major influence in my life. And I remember hearing her say hundreds, thousands of times, 'You don't have to work that hard to try to be a good person, just do it.' Before 'just do it' was fashionable.**"
- **Oprah Winfrey:** On January 29, 1954, Oprah Gail Winfrey was born to unwed, teenage parents in Kosciusko, Mississippi. Oprah had a mountain of obstacles already in front of her as a newborn baby. She was born to unwed teenage parents, she was female, she was black, and she was poor. Oprah's mother was an eighteen-year-old housemaid named Vernita Lee. Her father was a twenty-year-old doing duty in the armed forces: his name was Vernon Winfrey.
  For the first six years of her life, the young Winfrey was raised on a Mississippi farm by her grandmother. This was perhaps the first stroke of good luck for the young child. Oprah has stated that living with her grandmother probably saved her life. While in her grandmother's care, she was taught to read at a very early age, instilling a love of reading in her that she retains today. She began her public speaking career at the tender age

of three when she began reading aloud and reciting sermons to the congregation of her church. Oprah has said that she heard her grandmother state on several occasions that Oprah was "gifted." While the young child didn't know exactly what being "gifted" meant, she thought that it meant that she was special. And that was enough to keep her going.

- **Tom Hanks**: Born in California, Tom Hanks grew up in what he calls a "fractured" family. His parents were pioneers in the development of marriage dissolution law in that state, and Tom moved around a lot, living with a succession of step-families. No problems, no abuse, no alcoholism, just a confused childhood. He had no acting experience in college and, in fact, credits the fact that he couldn't get cast in a college play with actually starting his career. He went downtown, auditioned for a community theater play, was invited by the director of that play to go to Cleveland, and there his acting career started.

These are just a few examples of turnaround and individual success stories of well-known personal brands. The common link for all these great leaders and celebrities was their determination to not let their label or circumstances limit their ability to become great. Instead they used their label to propel them to shine.

There are circumstances where an early label can overtake your personal brand and thus you become that label. A great example is Shirley Temple.

- Growing up Shirley Temple was labeled and marketed as "the innocent kid." I can imagine this was a tough label to have as a kid, and that there was much pressure during her childhood and career to live up to this label. Today, Shirley Temple is not only remembered as the innocent little kid who became a hit star at age six, her namesake is also the name of a popular non-alcoholic beverage described by many as an innocent drink.

So ask yourself, are you a living example of your early label? Or have you spent your life disproving an expectation that others have pre-assigned to you? When I look back to my own personal experience, I can see a consistent life pattern that extends from being labeled "the oldest boy." The early leadership responsibilities that came with looking after my younger siblings helped prepare me for the personal and professional leadership roles that I have had during the course of my life and career. If there was one thing that

I would like you to take away from this chapter, it would be to fully embrace the notion that expectations matter.

The Expectation Lifecycle of Your Brand?

In the study of marketing management and branding, there is much focus on a product's lifecycle or PLC (see figure a). The PLC is the period from which a product is introduced, adopted through trial, matured through sustained brand positioning, and then declines or erodes due to new product entrants, competition in the marketplace, or changing trends.

Figure A
Marketing Product Lifecycle (PLC)

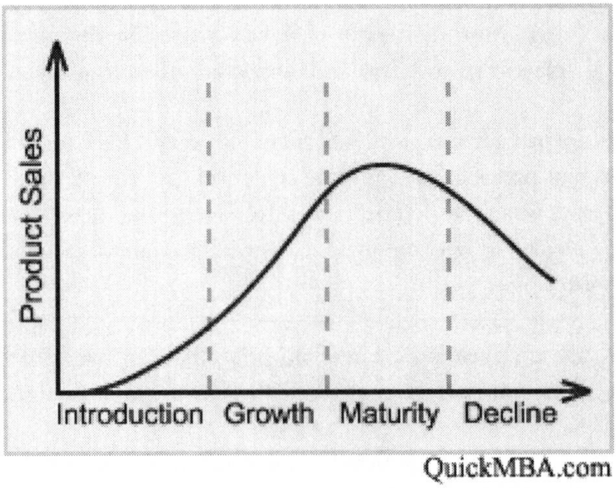

Good brands are able to sustain their brand positioning over long periods in the wake of fierce competition, new products, and changing consumer preferences and trends. Further, they are able to avoid brand erosion by constantly reinventing their packaging and their appeal to new and existing customers.

But have you ever thought about your life and what I call your expectation lifecycle? Please complete your answers to the questions below:

1. What do you think other people expect from you? ____________
   ____

2. What is your expectation lifecycle? In other words, what was your early childhood label and how does it compare to what others expect from you today?

   Early childhood label____________________________

   What others expect from you today__________________

   Your occupation ________________________________

3. How does what you internalized early in life relate to the personal brand you have established with others today?

   Write three words that describe the impression you wish to leave with others.

   ____________ _______________ ______________

4. **What do you aspire to be?**_________________________

Your ELC

Let's analyze your Expectation Life Cycle™ (ELC). Is there a correlation between your label, what others expect from you, the lasting impression you leave with others, and what you aspire to be? Take some time to reflect on what you wrote above. Are you a living example of your label? A living leader? A living legend? Or, a living list of reasons why your personal brand is misrepresented and under-expected?

Most people do not think of their life and career in this context. In fact, it is hard to conceptually think of yourself as a consumer product, especially if you accept the notion that products are bought, sold, consumed, and discarded. However, people are in fact bought, sold, consumed, and discarded, so learning to position yourself in this context will help you be the recipient of greater opportunities and reduce the opportunities that you are denied access to obtain today.

Think for a second about your career or life aspirations. Are there opportunities that you believe are being kept from you without your knowing just because others do not expect that you have the capabilities to exude something great?

For example, I remember a time early on in my career where I was really excited about research and using statistics to come to a conclusion on a business issue. I had been working in a group that consisted of four employees. Each member had a specific area of expertise that was brought together to form our project team. Given my marketing and advertising background, I was labeled "the creative one" in my group, and thus was the one called on to come up with marketing and communication strategies to sell our ideas to our internal stakeholders and position them to the press. The other three members of the team had expertise in credit analysis, legal issues, and research.

There was a really interesting project that was coming our way involving the analysis of consumer-generated data of shopping patterns. We were looking to identify certain behaviors amongst a group of existing customers that could help us build a predictive financial model to target them with new banking products. This was an exciting project, one that I eagerly looked forward to participating in and the opportunity to share more of my research and analysis skills.

As the project advanced, there arose a need for a member of our team to spend a month in another state analyzing patterns at retail store venues. The person selected would be responsible for developing an analytical report on statistical differences between shopper behaviors for in state customers versus those that lived out of state.

I wanted this assignment badly, and even campaigned by providing analytical reports for things I was not even asked to do. Every opportunity I got to speak to my supervisor I mentioned my interest in the new assignment and shared some data point, statistic, or percentage increase to show him that I was capable of handling the work that would be required. One day, a couple of weeks after I had put my request in for the assignment, I saw one of my team members arrive to the office with luggage and his computer. I asked him, "Hey are you going on vacation?" to which he replied, "No I am about to start the out of state assignment, wish me luck."

As you can imagine, I was disappointed, upset, dejected, discouraged, disheartened, and certainly disapproved of the decision. I was also upset that no one had told me that a decision was already made. I tried to mask my disappointment by wishing him luck, but it was obvious that I had just been passed over and it hit me like a truck. I left work that day questioning why I did not get selected and pondered over and over if there was something that I could have done differently.

The next morning I went in to my supervisor's office and asked him to tell me why I was not selected for the assignment. He looked at me and smiled and said, "You are just too good at marketing. I wanted our research person to handle this because I am sure he can get it done faster. We are on a tight schedule." I looked at him and told him thanks for the explanation and in the next breath mentioned that I too had former educational training in statistical analysis and would love to be considered next time for an opportunity like this one.

When I think back to that day I realize what upset me the most was that I internalized the words of my supervisor to say, "I think someone else can do it better than you." Although this was exactly what he was saying, the reality of the situation was that I did not prepare him to know what I was fully capable of delivering, and thus it was too late by the time the assignment came available to change his perceptions of me and my capabilities. So in essence, I was underexpected. Today, I still treasure this experience as one of my greatest lessons learned about the importance of shaping impressions and managing perceptions that others have of you.

Expectation management is a skill that when managed well will give you an advantage to avoid being passed over for opportunities. So here are some tips on how to effectively manage expectations.

1. Have an expectation agreement

In life we sign agreements to do just about everything. The higher the value of the item we are expecting to receive, the more comprehensive the process to confirm the agreement. When you buy a house and sign mortgage papers, you may sign up to one hundred pieces of paper just to say "yes I want to buy the house." The same goes for buying a car or an insurance policy. For each of these items because you expect to receive something of high value, you expect to have an agreement. Apply this same thinking to your life and career.

For everything that you seek to obtain, want to be considered for, or expect to receive, if you do not have an expectation agreement in place with the grantor of the opportunity, you should not expect to receive what you desire. In an expectation agreement you are simply stating to a mutual party that which you are looking to achieve, so that they have a clear understanding that you should be considered when the opportunity arises to achieve it. When you have an expectation agreement in place it also shows that you place a high value on your personal brand.

2. Understand the difference between expectation and entitlement

Just because you believe you are entitled to something does not mean you should expect to achieve it. Many professionals believe that their title entitles them to expect certain opportunities to come their way. While some titles do come with immediate certainties of opportunity, a title does not entitle you to expect opportunity. Opportunities will come from how you manage your personal brand. When you understand the difference between expectation and entitlement you will understand that personal or professional advancement is gained by working hard to create your opportunities.

Further, your ability to build connections with others and establish a solid reputation for already doing well in the past the things you want to achieve in the future will drive your ultimate success. When you have proven yourself you can expect to achieve opportunities to advance. Without a proven track record you are not entitled to expect to achieve the opportunities that come from having one.

3. Tell others what to expect before they expect it

Just as the early bird gets the worm, the first person to share what to expect gains an advantage in driving a desired perception. Before you enter a room to speak, before you go on an interview for a job or position, before you schedule a meeting or conference call, let people know what they should expect. By doing so you will set everyone's expectations to align with what you are looking to achieve. So in essence, you are preparing yourself to win by influencing the preconceived perceptions that would otherwise happen by chance.

This is a powerful strategy when you believe you are facing preconceived opposition or bias. For example, I have a friend who has dreadlocks and was applying for a job with a company that had a rigid corporate culture. Although he had a stellar resume, excellent grades in school, and solid prior work experience, he expected to face opposition when it came to his dreadlocks. He knew that his dreadlocks would be a stumbling block and barrier in his interview process.

In helping him prepare for the interview, I encouraged him to reach out to the person who would be interviewing him and let that person know that he had dreadlocks. I further advised him to go to the office of the company where he was interviewing one day in advance of the interview and sit in the lobby to watch how the people who were entering and leaving the building were dressed. He took my advice and walked into the interview dressed in business attire, just like the current employees he saw entering the building the prior day.

During the interview he thanked the interviewee for allowing him to share in advance that he had dreadlocks and told a story of how his dreadlocks, while different, allowed him to see how people react to him naturally and gave him a true sense of which companies valued diversity. What the interviewer discovered in the interview was that he was a technical wizard and a leading computer programmer for several intelligence bureaus and aviation agencies. His technical skill was exactly what the company was looking for, but had exhausted months working to find a candidate with the skills he possessed. Weeks later he was offered the job and remained at that company for many years.

The lesson learned from this story is that he prepared to be successful in the interview by managing the interviewer's expectations in advance of the interview taking place. As a result he was able to reduce the barriers that could have led to his demise. When you tell people what to expect from you before they expect to hear it, you make it easier for them to form the right perceptions that align with your goals.

4. Make an appointment for an expectation check-up

When was the last time you confirmed that you were doing not just what was requested but what is expected? To manage expectations effectively, you must be vigilant to "check in" often and consistently with others to make sure you are both on the same page. Sometimes the chapters change, or the book gets put back on the shelf, or worst yet the book comes to the end before you have even read the table of contents. An expectation check-up should play like a card game and result in a matching up of three objectives and goals with another's three objectives and goals. If all cards match, then your appointment is over. Next patient!

5. Deliver against the expectations you set

If you don't deliver the goods, you won't reap the rewards. If others do not see, have, experience, gain, realize, or find value in what you are delivering, it will make it harder for you to set expectations going forward. Therefore, the expectations that you set will expire before they have any meaning in the minds of others.

Expectation management is about setting expectations before they are prescribed to you. It only works, however, when the expectations you set can be backed up with evidence and performance results. Do not set an expectation that you know you cannot deliver, do not make a promise that you know you cannot keep, do not refer someone who you do not personally believe is capable, and do not have someone represent your personal brand who you do not expect to fully deliver your personal value.

There are limits

While this chapter focuses much on managing expectations to avoid limitations, the reality is, limitations can and do exist when you are not successful at managing your personal brand. So here are some tips on overcoming limitations.

1. Limit your limitations

If you believe you have hit a wall, a rough patch, or a glass ceiling, remember that a limitation is only as true as you allow it to be. Limitations are barriers that are placed to prevent opportunity and success from happening. They get stronger and more real the closer they get to your mind. So you can limit your limitations by limiting the limitations that you allow to enter your mind. An effective way to do that is to feed your mind with the opportunity you want to achieve. In other words, talk to yourself.

I often get up in the morning and tell myself that it is going to be a great day. Sometimes this simple message is all it takes to set me on the path to a wonderful day and to overcoming any doubts or barriers that would prevent me from this outcome. So what does "you" say to "self"?

A great example of this is Lance Armstrong.

Facing testicular cancer and not yet knowing his own fate, in 1997 champion cyclist Lance Armstrong established the Lance Armstrong Foundation, a non-profit organization that inspires and empowers people affected by cancer. This marked the beginning of Lance's role as an advocate for cancer survivors and a world representative for the cancer community.

One of the world's best cyclists at the age of twenty-five, Lance's competitive nature helped him confront his diagnosis head-on as he called himself not a cancer victim, but a cancer survivor.

As a record-holding, seven-time winner of the Tour de France, Lance's story gives hope and strength to people affected by cancer. A leading advocate for cancer survivors, Lance was appointed to serve on the President's Cancer Panel, an advisory group that reports directly to the President about Americans and cancer.

With his continued involvement with the Lance Armstrong Foundation and the cancer community, Lance serves as a constant reminder that in the battle with cancer, unity is strength, knowledge is power, and attitude is everything.

Lance's attitude allowed him to limit his limitation and focus on his life goals which were to win cycle races.

2. Ask for feedback and accept criticism

When you ask for feedback you begin to exterminate the negative elements of the things that hold you back. Feedback is a remedy for limitation and will help you gain access to the keys to opportunities' door.

3. **Change please**

Change preserves progress and keeps your spirit moving in a direction that creates growth. We seldom monitor the change we undergo in our personal brand, but a focus on how we are growing through change will direct our actions to be the change we want to see and the results we aspire to achieve. Pick a routine that you believe is limiting you from the opportunity to advance your life and your career and change it.

4. **Give someone an appraisal**

How often do you raise your brand by showing appreciation for others? A simple unsolicited "thank you" can go a long way to building a positive personal brand with others and getting over the limitation you feel within yourself. We often don't pay enough attention to the people who we most need to thank, and in doing so, we become thankless ourselves. A great way to overcome your limitations is to find something positive in someone else and tell them about it. As you lift their spirits you uplift yourself from the limitation that holds you down.

5. **Act it out**

Opportunities are created by actions. Limitations are destroyed by actions. Actions determine outcomes. Outcomes leave impressions. Impressions set expectations and create your personal brand. Think for a second on the previous set of sentences and what you do each day to create opportunities as a result of the impressions you leave with others. To overcome limitations, focus on creating your own opportunities by having a clear plan. Your plan should connect your actions to the outcomes they develop for your personal brand to shine. Each day, list one action you will take to get yourself closer to meeting a specific goal. List one outcome that will derive from your actions and define the impressions you want to leave as a result of them.

Get on Your KASE

KASE™ is a concept I developed that stands for **K**now, **A**ssess, **S**elf-**E**xpress. This is the business case for your personal brand, or your personal brand rationale. I coined this term because I wanted to give you an easy way to think about your personal brand and how to identify it. This exercise will lead you to a quick and comprehensive understanding of your living personal brand today. It is simple and will give you a framework for shaping "brand you."

So here's an exercise I would like you to try at home. It may be difficult, but try to give an honest depiction of yourself and get an honest answer from the friends you ask to participate. I call this the KASE exercise.

Exercise:

Write down three words that describe what you think you are known for.

1. ______________________________
2. ______________________________
3. ______________________________

Now ask a friend or colleague to tell you three words that in their eyes you are most known by.

1. ______________________________
2. ______________________________
3. ______________________________

Once you have confirmed your six words, stack them side by side. Now write a sentence about yourself that combines all six words and demonstrates the mix of what you think you are known for and what you are probably really known by.

Let's look at your KASE

____

____

____

____

Here's an example of my KASE:

Words I think I am known for	Words friends know me by
Talented	Saxophone
Professional	Successful
Creative	Approachable

Now if I were to write a personal statement sentence that combined all six words and demonstrated the mix of what I think I am known for, and what I am most known by, it would look something like this.

Example One: Kaplan is a talented and creative professional who in addition to being successful in business, plays the saxophone and is very approachable.

Example Two: Kaplan is a professional saxophone player and a talented, creative individual who happens to also be successful and approachable.

Example Three: Approachable, successful, and a talented creative professional who plays the saxophone, that's Kaplan Mobray

Go back to the sentence you wrote above to depict your KASE. Does your sentence reflect the real you? Are there words that you were given that you do not necessarily want as a part of your personal brand? If so, let's try again. Write a new KASE sentence for yourself incorporating the words you want used to define your personal brand.

____

____

____

____

Your walking personal brand; the unfiltered personal brand that you are today in the minds of others, is the convergence of the six words you have written from your KASE exercise above. Unfortunately, you do not get to choose the right side of the equation, and so you may end up with words, attributes, and adjectives that others use to describe you that you do not want associated with your personal brand.

Conclusion

Managing expectations is an essential skill for managing your personal brand. Having an awareness of what others expect from you, and how to manage the expectation of what you can deliver, will help you to be more proactive in living up to the brand you carry so that it is consistent with the brand you want to convey. When you have an awareness of what others expect from you, and focus on managing expectations in advance, you will help yourself to become the keeper of your personal brand. I would suggest you read this chapter twice and keep it as a reference guide for shaping Brand You.

When you know what others expect from you, you can decode the surveillance equipment that others use to assign you a brand.

Chapter 10K

Know Why You Are Doing What Your Are Doing Today and How it Will Shape Where You Are Headed Tomorrow

In This Chapter

- Why you do what you do?
- Personal brand planning

Why do you do what you do?

Have you ever really stopped to think about why you are doing what you are doing today? And how it will shape where you are headed tomorrow? Most people relate what they are doing today to a specific need they have for tomorrow. Think about your current job, occupation, or life situation. Have you ever asked yourself the following questions?

1. Why am I doing this?
2. If you were not doing your job or occupation, what would you be doing to fulfill your life?

Your answer to the second question is most likely the thing or goal that you are working to obtain. We all want to do the things that bring us life fulfillment and as a result we strive to accept and make sense of the delayed gratification in our life which we often call "work." Work is a means to a concrete goal, and a product of being committed to the journey of obtaining life and career fulfillment. Today you may be overly focused on the "need" to work as the driving force behind what pushes you in your career. In doing so you may also overlook the "need" to fulfill your life as the ultimate mission of your existence.

This impetus behind human motivation can be found in Maslow's Hierarchy of Needs, *Abraham Maslow (1954).*

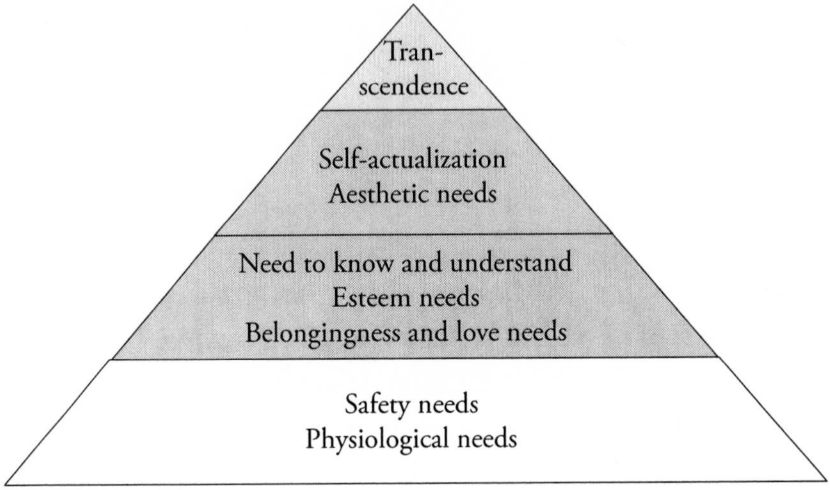

Maslow states that humans have a core set of needs that must be met in order for growth and self-actualization to occur. These needs include:

1) **Physiological:** hunger, thirst, bodily comforts, etc.
2) **Safety/security:** out of danger
3) **Belongingness and Love:** affiliate with others, be accepted
4) **Esteem:** to achieve, be competent, gain approval and recognition
5) **Cognitive:** to know, to understand, and explore
6) **Aesthetic:** symmetry, order, and beauty
7) **Self-actualization:** to find self-fulfillment and realize one's potential
8) **Self-transcendence:** to connect to something beyond the ego or to help others find self-fulfillment and realize their potential

I relate Maslow's theory to the 10th K by suggesting the following:

In order for one's personal brand to be fully realized, there must be a destination where the goal of branding yourself can be met with the results of life and career fulfillment. In other words, when you actively manage your personal brand, you know exactly where you want your personal brand to take you, and how you will use your brand to get you there.

It takes planning and focus to know where you are headed in life and in your career. It takes reflection and perspective to know why you do what you do today. But, it takes courage to admit you don't have a clue. For many of us, although we inherently have an idea of what we are doing today, we often times do not connect it to where we want to be tomorrow or at the very least, we do not write it out for ourselves to see. Just like signing contracts, however, the things we put in writing, are the things to which we direct our focus. So why are you doing "what" you are doing today? And "how" will it shape "where" you are headed tomorrow? Let's explore this further by writing out your aspirations.

What are you doing with your life today? In other words, what is your personal mission, life situation, or current professional occupation?

Why are you doing this? What are the reasons that drive you to do what you do?

What are three things you do each day to keep you on track to achieve what you aspire to be?

Your aspirations and dreams are a collection of actions that you take each day to reach a personal or professional milestone. As you relate your responses to the questions above to the outcomes you are experiencing in life, you will see that understanding "the reason why" is just as important as knowing "the expectation of." In other words, when you are actively aware of your actions, behaviors, thoughts, decisions, beliefs, values, contributions, performance, failures, faults, achievements, and expectations, you can actively embrace the consequences and results of each of these elements of your life.

When you embrace these elements of your life, you can then seek the outcomes that you experience as a result of your expectations. Personal branding is really about planning for the outcomes you want to happen for your life and career. My dad used to always say, "When you fail to plan, you are planning to fail." This phrase helped serve as a reminder about the importance of planning for success and today it has helped me to prepare for the things that I want to have in life and the legacy I want to leave as a result of living. So what do you want to have in your life? What do you want to leave as your legacy for living?

Personal Brand Planning

Personal brand planning will prepare you to better answer these questions and to live a life that is focused on not just talking about but rather obtaining your life goals. While this type of planning is not easy, it can become easier when you incorporate activities and behaviors that you conduct daily and relate them to your personal brand. Here are a few for you to consider.

Mail yourself a monthly bill for what you aspire to be

At the start of every month when you are mailing out letters and paying bills, mail a letter to yourself that lists what you aspire to be. As you get in the habit of writing to yourself, you will reinforce your commitment to pursuing your goals and keep yourself accountable when you lose focus. Everyone likes to get mail, but most people do not mail themselves a letter. Try it, and see for yourself how it will motivate you to turn your aspirations into accomplishments.

Make a shopping list for personal brand attributes

Each month when you put together your shopping list for groceries, add one product for your personal brand. Select a product that will enhance your personal appearance, enrich your mood, or a product that will simply allow you to increase an area of performance. As you incorporate items for your personal brand on your list of brands to shop for, you will help shape where you are headed tomorrow and stock up on the most important brand on your list, "Brand You."

Schedule an appointment for a personal brand checkup

Whether you have scheduled a doctor's appointment, brought your car in for a tune-up, or have had a mid-year performance review at your job; when you schedule a checkup, you give yourself a status update on your progress toward a specific goal. To shape the direction of your personal brand it is important to schedule regular check-ins where you can assess the strength of your brand, the perception you are leaving with others, and gather evidence that confirms your value.

I schedule my check-ins during my daily afternoon run in the park. It is this activity where I find myself reflecting the most about the day that has passed, the week that is ahead, and where I pump myself up to continue living my brand. Find the place or venue that works for you, just remember to check-in for your personal brand checkup.

Take your personal brand on vacation

Focusing on yourself, your goals, the impression you leave with others, and the actions you take to reach your goals is not always fun and it is sometimes exhausting. It is important to charge your battery by learning a new skill, traveling to a place you have never been before, and speaking to someone from a country or ethnic background you have never engaged. When you put yourself in a new environment you awaken your senses and the part of your mind that looks to create meaning. You also replenish your desire to learn and grow, thus charging your personal brand battery. If you are always on "E" you won't get to "F." Find ways to reinvent yourself, take on new challenges, and become more efficient. As you do you will fuel your brand with the energy, enrichment, and enthusiasm that motivates you to continue pursuing your goals.

Conclusion

I encourage you take these concepts; the 10Ks of Personal Branding principles, and begin to incorporate them into the areas of your life where you devote the most focus and attention. By doing so, you will begin to live each day with a daily reminder of the importance of building your personal brand and living your life by a true decision not by default. Life is precious and unpredictable, so you owe it to yourself to live the best version of your life while you are alive to do so. Personal brand planning and preparation will help you to meet your goals head-on and with greater results.

When you have a purpose, people see it! When you have a goal, you work to meet it! When you know "why" you are doing "what" you are doing today, and how it shapes "where" you are headed tomorrow, you are likely to succeed.

Special K

Know How to Ask For What You Want

In This Chapter

- Asking is confidence
- The science of asking

Asking is confidence

How comfortable are you asking for what you want? You may be surprised to know that although many people know what they want in life, people are generally afraid to ask for what they want. This is often driven by a preestablished fear of the outcome of asking for something. Generally people are just as afraid to succeed as they are to be rejected. The fear of rejection, however, is the number one reason people do not get what they want in life. Furthermore, ninety percent of the things we fear never happen.

Confident people ask for what they want. They ask for what they want out of others, and for what they want out of themselves. Being able to ask for what you want is a very important tool in building your personal brand. While your personal brand is built based on the expectations that others have of you, it starts with the expectation you set for yourself. This in many ways is a result of asking yourself for something and expecting to get it. When you expect to get what you ask others to give, you have created a mindset focused on achieving your goals. Surprisingly much of achieving goals is simply building up the courage to ask for them.

However, the big questions when it comes to asking, are will you ask? How will you ask? And what should you ask for? Many people do not achieve their goals because they do not know how to ask for the things that they want, need, or desire. They are fearful of asking for help, information, directions, or assistance. They are fearful of asking for a job, money to finance a project, help to meet a project deadline, a date, or a pay raise that would make the rest of their life better.

Rejection is not something that happens to you, it is something that you give to yourself. It is important when you want something to believe you are good enough to get it instead of assuming that you are not going to get it. Otherwise the rejection occurred way before you asked the question.

Asking is confidence and an amazing release. Asking affects everything else. It affects your body posture, your eye contact, the tone of your voice, your mental balance, your mannerisms, and even your choice of words. When you ask with an expectation that you will get that which you're asking for, your way of being gets into alignment with the things you are looking to achieve. In other words, you become the things you ask for.

So what are the opportunities and goals in your life that you have been holding yourself back from achieving simply because you have not asked? Please write your responses on the lines below.

Who are the people in your life or profession who are not benefiting today from the capabilities that you can deliver because you have not asked?

If you had only one thing to ask of yourself, what would it be?

Whatever it is you want, start by asking and expect that you will get it. Asking is not an easy thing to do. It takes courage and an acceptance that you may not get what you ask for. In essence, you have to be courageous enough to accept rejection before you ask for anything. The interesting thing about asking for opportunity is that when you "ask," you position yourself to "receive." At the same time, you build confidence because asking allows you to overcome a personal barrier in the process.

The confidence you gain from asking also helps strengthen your personal brand. The more confidence you create in your life the easier it is to know how to ask for what you want. So think about how and when you ask for what you want today or the many opportunities that you have avoided simply because you did not know how to ask for what you want.

The Science of Asking

Here are some tips on asking that will help you begin to receive the opportunities you truly desire and deserve.

Step One: Have a game plan for knowing what you want. Make a "want" list.

If you don't know what you want, you won't know when you've achieved it.

When it comes to your life and your career, what do you want? If you cannot answer this question you may never know when you've been successful. In fact, you might achieve what you thought you wanted without even knowing it. So to know what you want you must first understand the things that you would regret not having accomplished, obtained, achieved, or produced.

Exercise

Take out a blank sheet of paper. List as many things as possible that you have not done in your life or career that you would regret not doing if you suddenly died today.

Write down to the best of your ability everything that comes to mind. Don't stop writing and don't censor your responses or even think too hard about anything. Just write. You might find some crazy things or even private things you have never shared with anyone coming out of the end of your pen, and that's okay. Let them be. Just write. It is important to understand the things that you would regret not doing or having as a basis for knowing what you want.

After you have completed your list, find a place or room that you visit often and post your list there so you have a visual reminder of the things you want. Perhaps you may want to post it on your refrigerator, or on top of your bathroom mirror, or next to your bed or computer. Find a place where your list can stare at you every day. As you take time over the next few days and weeks to look at your list, begin to notice the things that you feel the most sense of urgency to accomplish or obtain. In fact, pick out your top three wants from your list. These are the things that you "want now" and are willing to sacrifice other regrets to obtain. This is an important exercise, because in life we want many things, but achievement is about focus.

After you have identified your top three wants, write them down below and answer the following questions.

My top three "wants."

1. ______________________________

2. ______________________________

3. ______________________________

Why do you want these things?

____

____

____

____

How will you benefit from receiving what you ask for?

____

____

____

____

How will the provider of what you ask for benefit from giving it to you?

____

____

____

____

What is the consequence of not receiving what you ask for?

____

____

____

____

To actively know what you want you must also know why you want "it," how you will benefit from achieving "it," how whoever gives "it" to you will benefit, and what would be the consequence of not receiving "it." This process will give you a complete understanding of the value of your want with respect to your life and career circumstances. The reason it is important to factor the other considerations into your want is because people do the same thing when building a perception of your personal brand.

When you are in a situation where opportunity can be gained, like in a job interview, people do not just want to offer you a job. They want to know why they should offer you the job, how they will benefit from having you as an employee, how you will be personally and professionally challenged through your role, and what the opportunity gain or loss would be if they did not hire you. When you understand this as the process of how people make a selection for the things they want, you can better position yourself to achieve the opportunities you seek.

So the next time you go for a job interview or opportunity exchange, read this section and use this framework to prepare yourself to ask for the opportunity. It will help you to position the things you want to achieve from that exchange with the selection process that others will be using to determine if they want you.

Step Two: Position your "ask" in the context of giving, not getting.

Think for a second about how you react to people who want to sell you something. Now think about how you perceive people who ask if their product or service can be of help to you in any way. While these two scenarios are different, they both have the same intent; asking for opportunity.

Many people ask for something with the sole focus on their own personal gain. A common question for people who think this way is, "what will I get out of this"? While you may not say this phrase directly when asking for an opportunity, people generally can tell if you are trying to "sell" them as opposed to trying to "help" them. If you are only focused on selling when asking someone for something you may well be denied what you are asking for solely because of your style.

As it relates to your personal brand, if you are only focused on selling yourself without positioning yourself as an asset, you may also be denied the very things you are looking to achieve. So here are some asking strategies to position any ask in the context of giving, not getting.

a. Warm the crowd before you give the punch line

Before you ask for what you want you must establish why you are relevant. People need to know why you matter, why they should listen to you, why you are a credible source, and how your capabilities can help them become better.

b. Give someone a reason to like you before you ask them to buy you

People buy products that they like or are told they should like. Give people a reason to like you. A smile, a reference, a greeting on behalf of a mutual acquaintance, a gift, or an unexpected surprise all help people think favorably about you. When people like you, they form positive impressions about your willingness and capabilities to help them succeed. It is always easier to get what you want from a cheerful giver. Jeffrey Gitomer, author of *The Little Red Book of Selling,* puts it this way: "If you make a sale, you can earn a commission. If you make a friend you can earn a fortune."

c. Feed before you are fed

Whether it is lunch, dinner, coffee, dessert, brunch, linner, cocktails, or pizza, food is a common denominator among people. When you feed someone or engage in conversation over a meal that you pay for, you give that person personal and professional nourishment. People remember people they eat with and usually remember them in a more positive light than those whom they have not interacted with over a meal.

An article by Larry Jacoby and Colleen Kelley, published by the Society for Personality and Social Psychology, notes that, "Aware memory, such as recognition and recall, occurs when memory serves as an object of attention. Unaware memory occurs when memory serves as a tool to accomplish a present task."

In other words, when the relationship you build with someone is solely over the phone or e-mail, you are playing to their unaware memory which positions you to accomplish a task. When you feed someone, you cater to their aware memory by adding another dimension of how you make yourself memorable, which only strengthens the relationship with another person giving you permission for your ask.

As you think about getting the things you want in life and for your career, think about your approach. It's always easier to say no to someone whose interests do not represent some greater good or objective beyond personal gain. So as you think about asking for opportunities in your life and for your career, think about your ask in the context of, "If I get what I want, it will create opportunities for others." Another way to look at this is, "I am asking for X because in getting 'it,' I will have the opportunity to help create a better outcome for Y." Finally, you will master the science of asking by having no expectations.

Step Three: Expect nothing in return to gain everything up front.

When you least expect it, someone may actually listen to what you have to say. -Maggie Khun

One of the biggest mistakes people make when asking for something is not being prepared to hear the word "no." Most people have a preconceived expectation of what another person will deliver when asking for something. For example, I know people who have written blank checks based on the certainty of an outcome, and when that outcome did not end up as they had expected, they lose control and damage the relationships they established while asking for that opportunity.

Desperation is one of the worst human conditions, especially when it comes to selling one of the best personal products: you. When you expect nothing when asking for everything, you position yourself and your personal brand as having confidence in your product. Confidence when selling yourself or asking for opportunity is a valuable asset and a powerful approach. It positions you as someone who does not need the result of the "ask" but who *wants* to share the benefit of the ask to make someone or something better.

To get what you want in life and for your career, positioning is key. Take time to reflect on how you ask for opportunities today. Do you know what you want? Are you a giver or a taker? How much confidence do you have in your abilities so you are not seen as desperate? When you know how to ask for what you want, you will be much more successful in getting what you ask for.

The interesting thing about asking for opportunity is that when you ask, you position yourself to receive.

Building Your Brand

In This Section

- How to build a personal brand
- Understanding the attributes that make brands successful
- A guide for living your brand every day

So now that you have fully digested the 10Ks of Personal Branding, it's time to put these concepts into the framework of your life and your career, so that you can begin living as a brand.

In this next and final chapter, let's build your brand from the ground up. This chapter is devoted to taking the principles that make great brands successful and applying it to you, so you can transform yourself into your own logo, your own package, and your very own product. Upon completion of this chapter you should have a direct set of instructions on how to focus your actions, external appearance, behaviors, connections with others, and your mindset to build your personal brand.

I have outlined several steps to get you started on this journey. Let's start with the first step, understanding the relationship between consumer products and your personal brand.

Products and Personal Branding

Have you ever thought about the products you use every day and what they say about you?

Stop and think for a second about the following products listed below.

1. Running sneakers
2. Coffee
3. Can of soda
4. Candy bar
5. Automobile

6. Handbag
7. Camera
8. Toothpaste
9. Favorite sports team
10. Gasoline

Think about how you use, consume, purchase, wear, select, and experience these products as a part of your daily activities. Now take a moment and think specifically about what drives your purchase decisions for each product and to which brands you are most loyal.

Assignment Number One – Understand the brands you consume and what they say about you

The first step to living as a personal brand is to understand the brands you consume every day and how you make purchase decisions. By this I mean, take the *unconscious* decisions you make every day about the foods you eat, the coffee you drink, the clothes you wear, the stores where you shop, the hotels where you stay, the car you drive, the computers you buy, and the teams you root for and become *overtly conscious* of why you make them. This will help you to develop a context for how you manage your own personal brand.

People often make decisions about brands based on how they view themselves. For example, if you want to feel clean you buy products that emphasize clean as their strongest attribute. If you believe that you are fast, sleek, and sexy you buy a car that is fast, sleek, and sexy. If you think of yourself as being of superior quality, you buy a camera that is of superior quality. The point I am making is that you buy what you internalize yourself to be or what you aspire to become. In an article for Brandchannel.com titled, "Is Brand Loyalty Dead?," Dennis Balajadia noted: "In a world where our choices are increasing dramatically … YOU are what you buy!"

You are indeed what you buy. So if we relate this philosophy to your personal brand, you'll begin to understand that people view you as a product and they will select you based on how you make them feel about themselves or how you help them achieve what they aspire to become. This is the great myth about personal branding. While personal branding is a tool that helps you focus to achieve your life outcomes, the success of your personal brand is dependant on how your brand actually helps others. When you understand how you as a consumer select brands and products, you will have a clear picture of how to build your personal brand.

As I mentioned, personal branding is not as simple as saying this is who I am, or this is who I want to be. It is a discipline that comes with an understanding of the principles of branded products and how they apply to you. I am a student of brands and in fact study my own consumer behavior daily. I know why I buy the products I consume, why I root for my favorite sports teams, why I wear the clothes I wear, why I watch the television shows I watch, and most importantly what it all says about me. This perspective allows me to take the attributes of how I use product brands and apply them directly to how I live.

So let's go back to the list of products we discussed previously. I purposefully selected products I know the average consumer consumes or has experienced in some form at least once a day. Your first assignment is to track these products and write a clear rationale for why you select the brands you consume and what they say about you.

Product	**Brand you currently use**	**Why did you choose that brand?**	**What does this brand say about you?**
Running sneakers			
Coffee			
Can of soda			
Candy bar			
Automobile			
Handbag			
Camera			
Toothpaste			
Favorite sports team			
Gasoline			

Take a look at your responses and reflect a moment on what your use of each product says about you across each product category. You should be able to see connections between your individual responses.

The similarities that you uncover in this exercise will indicate the strongest attributes of your personal brand and perhaps unconscious signals that you may be giving off when encountering others. For example, my favorite professional sports teams in the U.S. are the New York Yankees in baseball, the Los Angeles Lakers in basketball, and the San Francisco Forty Niners in football. When you add up the winning percentages of these teams they represent the winningest teams in their respective sport based on championships won over the past several decades. I choose to root for these teams because I admire their brand. Collectively, these teams represent a relentless dedication to winning and excellence. When I look at what I aspire to be, I can see myself, my values, and my brand clearly through these teams. What this says about me is that I am someone fully committed to winning and to delivering quality performance in whatever I do. So my personal values and the brand of the teams I root for are totally aligned, thus making me a loyal fan.

Let's take it back to the exercise we did in chapter 1K where I asked you to think of something that defined you without using your name. The brand name that I give myself when I cannot use my name is "Inspire." So to put it all together into a brand statement that demonstrates how I consume products and what it says about me, I would say, "I am inspired by winning and excellence in performance."

This example demonstrates how this first assignment is supposed to work. Now it's your turn. Write a similar sentence about yourself using the responses you provided. Pick one of your favorite brands, write down why you chose that brand as a favorite brand, then write down what you think it says about you. It's okay to be honest. Just write.

My favorite brand is ________________,

I choose or use this brand because____________________________

What this brand says about me is______________________________

My brand name from the name exercise is "____________________
____."

If you are not aware of the reasons behind your purchase decisions for the brands listed above, you may have been tempted to dismiss the relevance of this exercise to your personal brand. However, the reality is there are clear conclusions that can be drawn from your everyday purchase behavior that will help you better understand yourself.

I know what you're saying. How did gasoline end up on this list? Of all the products listed above, you probably have spent the least amount of time thinking about why and how you purchase gasoline, perhaps other than price. Your response to how you purchase gasoline does in fact indicate attributes that are present in your personal brand. For example, here are some common factors that influence the purchase of gasoline.

1. I purchase gas at the nearest gas station
2. I only buy gas from one brand
3. I purchase gas from the station selling it at the least expensive price
4. I travel to another state to fuel my tank because gas is less expensive in that state
5. I don't drive, but if I did I would purchase a specific brand of gas for my automobile
6. I purchase gas based on what provider is most environmentally friendly

Here's an example of how your purchase behavior may relate to your personal brand.

Purchase behavior	Personal brand attributes
I purchase gas at the nearest gas station regardless of price.	Your personal brand is shaped by conveniently adapting to the situation at the time.
I only buy gas from one brand.	You build strong affinity to perceived quality and hold for yourself a high standard for your personal brand and how it is perceived by others.
I purchase gas from the station selling it at the least expensive price.	Your personal brand is shaped by taking the easiest path to a stated objective.
I travel to another state to fuel my tank because gas is cheaper in that state.	A strong attribute of your personal brand is your focus on overcoming barriers. You never accept "no" for an answer.
I purchase gas based on what brand I believe is the most environmentally safe.	Your personal brand is shaped by a conscious effort to better your personal surroundings and the environment you create for others.

Okay, so this example may or may not apply to you, and if you are struggling to find the correlation, think about a product you use most and apply it to the same scenario. The point I am making is that to practically build your personal brand, you must think about how the decisions you make about brands affect your outlook. Your outlook will give you an approach to life and to your career that will help you focus specifically on messages and impressions you want to leave with others. These impressions are based on how you view your actions in connection to their impact, and what they say about you.

Assignment Number Two – Give yourself a brand name and define your brand contribution

So here's assignment number two. Now that you have established the foundation between how you make purchase decisions and what they say about you, let's connect the elements of a solid brand to specific behaviors that will help you shape your personal brand. Let's explore the 10K Branding Personal Brand Builder (PBB).

Personal Brand Builder™

The personal brand builder is an association map that will help you translate consumer product attributes to attributes of an effective personal brand. The more you can correlate these attributes across each spectrum, the greater your knowledge of what you need to do to live as a brand. Let's explore further.

There are ten critical elements of a solid brand that correlate to your personal brand. They include:

Branding Attributes	**Personal Branding Attributes**
Product	Brand and Contribution
Packaging	Personal Appearance
Price	Quality
Placement	Accessibility
Performance	Impact
Interior design	Mindset
Taste	Experience
Durability	Consistency
Reviews	Reputation
Logo	Style
Bonus Attributes	
Category	Association

Advertising	Impression

Let's explore these further.

Product Versus Your Brand Contribution

Without using your name, pick a product, thing, persona, picture, or attribute that defines who you are. This is what I call your "Brand Name." Now select the contribution you believe you make to the world you live in or your workplace environment. This is what I call your brand contribution. For example, my brand name is "inspire." My contribution to the world and workplace environment is to provide inspiration to those who I encounter or interact with regardless of the setting.

Now it's your turn. What is your brand name and the contribution you deliver to your environment and surroundings? This is the first step to completing your Personal Brand Builder (PBB). List your brand name and brand contribution below.

Your Brand Name	**Your Brand Contribution**

People buy products, and are loyal to their favorite brands. The key principle here is to begin to position yourself as not just a person but a branded product with real attributes. This perspective will create a compass that directs your actions and your behaviors toward exuding the attributes of the brand you wish to live and the contribution you wish to make through the product "You."

Giving yourself a brand name and personal brand contribution serves a second purpose. It is a badge that you can wear daily to distinguish yourself from a crowd. Let's explore this further.

Most people go through life in search of how they can differentiate themselves from others. This is especially true when you are presenting yourself for an employment opportunity, when completing an application for admission to school or an institution of higher education, or when meeting someone for the first time, perhaps going on a date.

The most common mistake that you can make in these situations is to focus on presenting your capabilities without communicating your brand contribution. Most people focus on capability alone as a way to differentiate themselves from competition and in doing so may actually decrease their likelihood of achieving a favorable outcome. Here are some common words you hear most often as sound bites in a job interview. These are words and phrases used by people who focus on capability alone.

"I have done this …"
"I completed this course of study and earned this degree …"
"My accomplishments are …"
"I saved the company two million dollars in three years."
"I generated three hundred thousand dollars in new business."
"I created this new program …"
"I made a lot of money in the stock market."

All of the above statements do effectively communicate what one has done and indicates some future likelihood of success; however, for the most part, the above quotes are all capability statements. As I mentioned earlier, there is a difference between capability and contribution. In fact, presenting your capability without defining your brand contribution will end up commoditizing your personal brand attributes as opposed to differentiating your value.

Here's an example of what I mean by communicating capability versus contribution. Earlier in my career I had gone on several interviews for two similar jobs. I interviewed with an advertising agency for an account supervisor role leading a team of eight people and also interviewed for a job as head of marketing for a major division of a publishing company. Both jobs required that I present how I could help the account and division grow. Both jobs were also looking for someone with my marketing and brand background, so it seemed like a natural fit to pursue both opportunities simultaneously. I decided to interview for these two jobs on the same day. Here's how each interview played out that day.

Interview scenario one: Head of marketing for major publishing division

I walked into the room, established eye contact, met and warmly greeted the interviewer, and began to answer questions about my resume. I proceeded to share what my strengths were and what I could accomplish to help the division grow. I explained past programs that I created in former roles that were successful, and how I worked effectively with others in teams. I also let the interviewer know that I was rated a top performer each year. I candidly shared that one of my strengths was my ability to quickly get things done and that I was good with people. I closed the interview by restating my qualifications for the role, and that my background working in marketing made me an excellent candidate for the job. The interviewer thanked me for coming in and said they would get back to me in a couple of weeks.

Interview scenario two: Account supervisor at advertising agency for high profile account

I walked into the room, established eye contact, extended a hand to warmly greet the interviewer, and began to answer a few basic questions. After about five minutes had passed I asked if I could take a moment to provide some additional background on myself. I knew that they had looked at my resume prior to me coming in to the office, so I turned the resume over so the interviewer was now staring at a blank piece of paper. I told the interviewer that I was aware that the agency has recently lost two fifty million dollar accounts and that the agency's newest client was taking a huge risk by signing up with the agency. I explained that given the tenuous nature of the account relationship, they were looking for a leader, a creative visionary, someone who could help transform the perception of a demanding client to see the true value and professionalism of the agency staff. I also highlighted the service orientation of the agency as something the agency was looking to prove to the new client.

I proceeded to mention that my resume stated many qualifications and accolades that I have received in helping clients achieve their creative and business goals, but what a resume will never state is my ability to influence, inspire, energize, and truly uplift a brand to be a winner with consumers. I followed up to say that winning is something that you cannot write on a piece of paper, but it is a shared belief that you create. "I create winners, I inspire leaders, and with the opportunity to lead this account, I will shape a winning culture for the agency that will have the world's most esteemed brands lining up at the door to be served by this agency. That is why I am here and I would be happy to answer any other questions you would like to discuss." The interviewer smiled with that look like she had gone fishing and had just made a catch. They had no further questions, thanked me for coming, and told me that they would be in touch in twenty-four hours.

Let's reflect for a second on these two scenarios. Which job do you think I landed? In both scenarios I presented my capabilities and why I would be the best candidate. However, in the second scenario, I shared my capabilities in the context of the contribution I could make as a result of them. Oh, by the way, I got that job as an account supervisor in scenario two and they never turned the resume back over.

The key takeaway here is that there is a difference between capabilities and contribution. When you can effectively position your capabilities in the context of the contribution you will make as a result of them, you will truly differentiate yourself and the product called "You."

Assignment Number Three – Give Yourself an Outer Package

Packaging Versus Personal Appearance

Brands are first and foremost recognized by their packaging. When you look at a Snickers bar you see the same wrapper, when you drink a can of Coca-Cola, regardless of the country you are in, it is the same red can with white stripes. When you open a box from Tiffany's it is the same turquoise-colored box, and when you pick up a bottle of Poland Spring water, it is the same clear bottle with the green strip. A brand's package signifies trust. It inspires action, and sets the expectation for the experience you will have once you open the package to get to the product.

In some cases a brand's packaging is more important than the product inside. It is the first visual and tangible identifier of the promise of the product or service one will receive. Great brands also keep their packaging consistent. Many of the world's most regarded brands have had the same packaging for decades. It is the consistency of their packaging, combined with the performance of the product that keeps consumers loyal and influences their ability to buy more products.

Similarly, you as a personal brand will be recognized first and foremost by your personal appearance. This is especially true in professional, managerial, clerical, secretarial, sales, service, and military occupations. Researchers **R. Keith Schwer and Rennae Daneshvary** at The Center for Business and Economic Research, University of Nevada, Las Vegas, noted that maintaining an overall good appearance is more important for persons in professional, managerial, or sales occupations than respondents employed in other occupations.

A study published in the *Journal of Social and Personal Relationships* suggested that the opinions we form in the first few minutes after meeting someone play a major role in determining the course of the relationship. Michael Sunnafrank and Artemio Ramirez, authors of the study, studied 164 college freshmen over a nine-week period to test Sunnafrank's "predicted outcome value theory," which holds that we predict the future of a relationship as soon as we begin communicating with another person. For the study, the students were paired on the first day of class with another student of the same sex. The students were asked to introduce themselves to their randomly selected partner and talk for either three, six, or ten minutes. After the conversation, they were asked to predict whether their future relationship would be one of nodding acquaintance, casual acquaintance, acquaintance, close acquaintance, friend, or close friend. They also filled out a variety of questionnaires about the person they had just met.

Over the next nine weeks, the classroom setting required them to interact with other students, rather than just listen to a lecture, thus providing plenty of opportunity to discover new things about their classmates. At the end of the nine weeks, partners who had rated each other positively had the strongest friendships, thus establishing the predictability of that first encounter.

If first impressions really do matter the most, then that first meeting ought to have a predictable impact, and the researchers say they found that to be the case. In fact, even after the students had been compelled to interact with each other over a nine-week period, those first impressions still played a major role in foretelling the relationship between students who had been paired together at the beginning of the study.

Appearance Matters

These studies are among many that have been conducted on this topic. Your personal appearance is one of the most important details that contribute to your personal brand and how you are perceived. Your appearance is a visual and tangible identifier that also signifies trust, inspires action, and sets the expectation for the experience others will have from an encounter with you, "the product." You may not realize it, but people make assumptions of your capability, quality, preparedness, and professionalism, credibility, and worth based on your personal appearance. You could include a number of additional factors that make this statement true.

In addition to the studies, there have also been many human experiments on this topic. One such human study, reported in 1972 in the *Journal of Personality and Social Psychology*, tested a hypothesis to determine what effect physical appearance plays on one's evaluation of another's performance. It was concluded that individuals attribute more positive qualities and expect better performance from physically attractive people than from physically unattractive ones.

The study, conducted by researchers David Landy and Harold Sigall of the University of Rochester, Rochester, N.Y., further suggested that "If you are ugly, you are not discriminated against a great deal so long as your performance is impressive. However, should performance be below par, attractiveness matters." They concluded that a beautiful person may be able to get by with inferior work because others expect that attractive people will perform well and therefore give them the benefit of the doubt when work is substandard or of dubious quality.

This is a remarkable finding and speaks volumes about the impact that your personal appearance has on how you are perceived. If you accept the underlying message from the study findings, you can interpret it to mean the better you look, the more people actually expect from you. This is a powerful statement as it relates to your personal brand because it also signifies that if you do not pay as much attention to your personal appearance, then others may dismiss you before you even get an opportunity to demonstrate your capability. In this case, the perception of you in the minds of others will be made well before they experience what you, "the product," can actually deliver.

What this indicates is that your "package," (your personal appearance), is actually just as important as your "product," (the capabilities you can deliver). Taking this a step further, in building your personal brand your "package" is actually your "product." The perception that you create from the first impression will signify your capability, your knowledge, your quality, your likeability, your worth, and determine your ability to influence others.

Cyber Looks

It is critical to note that this is not just relegated to your physical appearance but applies to your online appearance as well. There are millions of Web sites today competing for the same consumer's attention and eventual dollars. The Web sites that have an appealing personal appearance are the Web sites that attract a greater share of unique and repeat visitors and have a higher business transaction volume as a result. If you are a business owner, does your Web site truly convey your personal brand?

According to Worldbestwebsites.com, a Web site ranking authority of World Best Enterprises, a division of Creative Management Consultants, Inc., the personal appearance of a superior Web site should have:

- Visual appeal using exceptional artistry
- Professional appearance having an elegance and sophistication of core design elements
- Artistic integration incorporating clever synergies of visual elements and color harmonies – effective use of color, typography, and font styles
- Ease of use offering useful tools, helpful resources, simple navigation

Your personal appearance online is just as important as your personal appearance physically. So now that I have made you think about your personal appearance and how critically important it is to establishing credibility with others, here's what you can do to create a winning personal brand package, one that will inspire loyalty, action, and will dramatically influence how you are perceived.

Step One: Pick a logo that signifies your style

To do this, go back to the brand name you gave yourself at the start of chapter 1K and the beginning of this chapter. Take that word and translate it into a personal appearance style that associates you, your brand name, and your personal brand contribution. For example:

Brand Name	Style	Logo
Inspire	Sharp	Lightning bolt
Happy	Bright	Sun
Determined	Bold	Hammer
Outgoing	Casual and relaxed	Green grass

By picking a logo, outlining your style and its association to your brand name, you will create a formula for visualizing how others see you or how you want to be seen. We often do not think of ourselves as logos, but when you transform yourself into a personal brand you unconsciously build a personal brand logo in the process.

I have listed my brand name (inspire), style (sharp), and logo (lightning bolt) above so you have a living illustration of what it means to have a logo. Think about what words you would list for your name, style, and logo above. I have listed other examples to help you grasp this concept.

Step Two: Go through your wardrobe and take an inventory of any risks to your personal brand.

Now that you have clearly defined your brand name, your style, and your personal brand logo, go through your closet. Take an inventory of your clothes to assess if you can adequately make your personal brand statement, one that signifies your style based on your current wardrobe. If yes, then start to think about the way you dress yourself based on the brand name, style, and logo you identified above. If your answer is no, and you see a disconnect between what you wear and what you want to leave as your personal brand statement, then take action by recreating your wardrobe based on your new perspective.

You will be amazed at how more focused you will be when you connect your outer package to how you feel about yourself and the message you want to send to others. As I mentioned, brands are first and foremost recognized by their packaging. You are first and foremost recognized by your packaging, and your outer package will influence how you are perceived.

Step Three: Create your personal brand package

There is a widely-held view that on average, people dress themselves according to how they feel about themselves on any given day. If you subscribe to this school of thought, then you may also believe that there are societal norms that influence what you may wear in a particular situation or venue. For example, an office culture, professional environment, creative environment, or recreational environment may dictate what you select from your wardrobe, and thus you are somewhat held captive to the environment that has dictated these norms.

With personal branding, your package should be a consistent approach to how you select your daily wardrobe based on your brand name, style, and logo. When you adopt this approach, you adapt your wardrobe to changing external environments but keep the same core style as a part of your package. For example, while I may wear a suit and an unusual tie to work in a corporate environment, I may wear jeans and an interesting pair of sandals in a recreational environment, and slacks and a unique button-down shirt in a casual environment. The common element that I portray in each of these distinct environments is the style of being "sharp." So my package always has the same elements:

- Sharply dressed
- Well-groomed and tailored
- Attention to detail with a specific emphasis on color and contrast
- Wardrobe conveys energy and radiance

So let's take the personal brand package diagram that we explored earlier and add the final element, a package. See the example below for reference to help you visualize this concept. Take a second to review the chart; can you see yourself somewhere in this diagram? Perhaps I've hit it right on and you can clearly see your style, your logo, and your current personal appearance package listed on the diagram below. If not, let's create your package.

Complete the open box below to begin outlining your package statement.

Brand Name	**Style**	**Logo**	**Package**
Inspire	Sharp	Lightning bolt	Sharply dressed, well-groomed and tailored. Attention to detail with specific emphasis on color and contrast. Wardrobe conveys energy and radiance.
Happy	Bright	Smiley face	Bright colors that draw people in. Jewelry that stands out. A smile is an everyday accessory to your wardrobe.
Determined	Bold	Hammer	Consistently dressed in dark, solid, bold colors with less use of patterns. Have one statement piece (jewelry, tie) that is a powerful identifier and says you are about business.
Outgoing	Casual and relaxed	Sun	Anything goes. Dress according to how you feel that day. Prefer loose than form-fitting. Default to blue jeans or khakis whenever possible. Prefer button-down shirt or blouse to wearing a suit.
Your Brand Name	**Your Style**	**Your Logo**	**Your Package**

While you may not have previously thought about this diagram when selecting your wardrobe, you now have an awareness of how to package your brand name, your style, your logo, and your package to create the perception that others have of you. This framework is essential to building your personal brand.

Use this diagram consistently to help you create the impressions you want others to have of you and thereby you will prepare yourself for success both personally and professionally in the process. So the next time you pick out something to wear, don't just look at your clothes as a suit, blouse, pants, shirt, shoes, or single articles of clothing. Look at what you are putting on as the outer package for your personal brand. You want to create for yourself an outer package that will make others want to unwrap you to find out all the good that's inside.

The key here is to become more conscious of your personal appearance and its connection to how you are perceived. Ultimately, people buy into your package as the first step to buying into you. Therefore, you are the package you create for yourself and your success may come based first on how you look. So try this new approach. Before you pick out your clothes each day, think about your brand name, your style, your logo, and the package elements you want to convey to leave a favorable impression. As your personal appearance becomes something you prepare for daily, you will be able to package yourself as a powerful personal brand every day.

Interior Design Versus Mindset

Assignment Number Four – Match your mindset to your package

The interior design of a product supports its ability to deliver on its attributes. Similarly, the mindset you carry as a part of your personal brand will support your ability to leave favorable impressions and deliver the messages you want to convey.

Think about the interior of your car. If you don't own an automobile, then think about the interior of your bedroom. When your car or room is dirty, filled with clutter, or disorganized, you may also feel cluttered and disorganized. This outlook may lead you to be more stressed, can cause health issues, or even lead you to a depressive state.

A great article, *The Psychology of Being Organized* by Teri Emmet, sheds some light on this topic. The article states, "Individuals who are organized in their personal lives most generally constitute efficient and organized employees in their work environments, succeed in their personal endeavors and are, more often than not, financially secure. Once an organizational state of mind is established, your status of efficiency in all areas of your life will ultimately benefit."

There is a profound psychological thread that binds all areas of your existence into one distinctive unit. A messy house filled with useless clutter is an abstract representation of many lives—also muddled with unnecessary debris that needs to be regrouped, set aside, hidden out of sight or, better yet, disposed of completely. Wasted thoughts, wasted energy, and wasted time all add up to wasted money.

In contrast, a well-kept home and yard tend to indicate a well-ordered existence in every area of your life, whether it is financial, emotional or physical. Human nature prescribes that the way you handle your household affairs is generally the same method of productivity you bring to the workplace and to society in general. Those who have little respect for their own possessions and authority at home usually have even less regard for the possessions or authority of others.

Finding yourself "off course" creates an emotional imbalance, resulting in a feeling of being overwhelmed. This "overwhelming feeling" triggers a significant panic reaction that generally results in prompting you to attempt to correct everything at once. So you rush back and forth from one chore to another, not completing anything, thereby temporarily losing focus on any one particular project. Consequently, nothing gets completed and a vicious circle begins.

Living such an indiscriminate lifestyle denies you the feeling of exhilaration and pride in completing any project. Look realistically at what is happening and what you are doing to yourself. Look at the time and energy you are spending yet receiving nothing in return. At best, you end up with a sloppy, half-completed job and feelings of personal guilt and failure over it because you know you could have done better.

Your mindset is an important element of your personal brand. When your mindset is not tuned to a positive channel or frequency, it may prevent you from engaging others, may impact how you package yourself, and may cause you to be passed over for opportunities because you are not presenting to others your best version of yourself.

Now, I know it is a big stretch to make the connection from having a dirty room or messy yard to not landing a job, but the reality is, your mindset shapes your outcomes. When you can shape your inner mindset to the way you package yourself externally you will bring harmonious balance to your personal brand. Here's an example.

Bad Hair Day

Let's take the six words you most hate to say about yourself. "I'm having a bad hair day." What does this really mean? For sure there are days when we like the way our hair stands up or falls better than others. And if you don't have hair, then perhaps the way your forehead shines on a sunny day. Okay, bad joke! But what we are really saying to ourselves is that we do not like the way we feel inside as a result of how our packaging looks. Specifically, our mindset is affected by our package.

In building your personal brand you must match your mindset to your package so that your external package does not hamper your mindset and your mindset does not hamper your package. Rather, they both work harmoniously to give you a positive boost to support your personal brand. So select a mindset that depicts your personal brand.

Step One: Select a mindset that depicts your personal brand

So let's look at the Personal Brand Builder (PBB) below. What is the mindset that you associate with your brand name, your style, your logo, and your package? Begin to think about your mindset as you complete this example for your personal brand. I have provided some examples for reference.

Brand Name	Style	Logo	Package	Mindset
Inspire	Sharp	Lightning bolt	Sharply dressed, well-groomed and tailored. Attention to detail with specific emphasis on color and contrast. Wardrobe conveys energy and radiance.	Always optimistic. Can-do attitude at all costs. See the glass as half full. Seek to make a positive impact regardless of the circumstance. Brighten the outlook of others by accentuating positives and renouncing negatives.

Happy	Bright	Smiley face	Bright colors that draw people in. Jewelry that stands out. A smile is an everyday accessory to your wardrobe.	Approach each day with a smile. Remain open to possibilities. See the glass as half full. Brighten the outlook of others by accentuating positives and renouncing negatives.
Determined	Bold	Hammer	Consistently dressed in dark, solid, bold colors with less use of patterns. Have one statement piece (jewelry, tie) that is a powerful identifier and says you are about business.	Thoughtful and focused; Make to-do lists and check them off as a sense of accomplishment. Seek resolution to conflict. Start each day with a goal and end with record of your achievement.
Outgoing	Casual and relaxed	Sun	Anything goes. Dress according to how you feel that day. Prefer loose than form-fitting. Default to blue jeans or khakis whenever possible. Prefer button down shirt or blouse to wearing a suit.	Go along with the flow. Accept that there will be ups and downs. Look to fit in as opposed to stand out. Receive opportunities that come your way but don't put too much pressure on yourself to create them.

Your Brand Name	Your Style	Your Logo	Your Package	Your Mindset

Complete your mindset statement in the (PBB) chart above.

Having a conscious approach to your mindset as it relates to your personal brand will give you focus. It will help you stand up to the circumstances that life throws at you with an understanding of why and how you react to situations. It will also help you to better communicate the attributes of your personal brand that shape your outlook. Your mindset is an important part of your package and will allow people to genuinely see and buy into you which will build loyalty and trust. It's important when thinking about your mindset to realize that it is an outlook that you select not one that happens to you. When you "select" your mindset you are making a conscious choice to live your brand.

Step Two: Understand what your mindset says about you

Now that you have selected a mindset to support your personal brand package, it is important to understand what your mindset says about you. Earlier in this book, in Chapter 9K, you wrote down your "KASE." If you recall, this was an exercise that listed three words that you think you are known for and three things you are most known by. You then used those six words in a sentence about yourself.

Now let's see how your KASE equates to your mindset. There should be a direct correlation between the six words you came up with and the words you depict as your mindset. If not, it's important to go back and assess the difference between how others perceive you and the mindset you selected for your personal brand. What you may find is that although you have an idea of what you think you are known for, your mindset may be shaping what you are actually known by.

Step Three: Create specific personal brand actions that derive from your mindset

If you can visualize a tube of toothpaste, you then know that the interior design of that tube encourages you to squeeze from the bottom to get the best results. Relating this to your personal brand, create specific actions that derive from your mindset. This approach will put the attributes of your personal brand into action and allow you to live your mindset. For example, my brand name and contribution is to "inspire." My mindset is to brighten the outlook of others by accentuating positives, renouncing negatives, and encouraging others to see and get more out of themselves. I have some specific actions that derive from this mindset.

1. **I schedule ten minutes each day for some form of personal inspiration.**

This could be reading an uplifting quote, listening to a favorite musical tune, or going out of my way to do something generous for someone.

2. **I pick a point in the day where I will take ten deep breaths.** Breathing helps calm my mind and allows my mind and body to refocus. Although we breathe involuntarily to sustain life, we often are not conscious of just how much refreshment we get from taking a voluntary breath of fresh air.

3. **I work out or engage in some form of physical exercise.** For me, exercise is as much a mental activity as it is physical. Exercise gives me energy and it is this energy that I recycle to create the energy I use to inspire others.

So as you think about your mindset and its connection to your personal brand, create a set of actions and behaviors that you will do to strengthen your interior design. As you do, you will shape your personal brand and insulate your mind from being thrown off course so that you are living a well-orchestrated plan for achieving your personal and professional aspirations.

Taste Versus Experience

Assignment Number Five – Give yourself a taste and define the experience you want others to have from consuming your personal brand.

If you were a food product, what type of food would you be? I know this is not something you think about every day and perhaps you have never asked yourself this question. But let's go there together. Let's imagine you were a food product. What would you be? Would you be a snack, a meal, an entrée, an appetizer, or a dessert? Would you be a product in a can? Would you be served in a large container? Or would you be in a wrapper? Would you be a liquid? Or would you be a solid product? Finally, what would the experience be for someone who consumed you?

I don't know about you, but all this food talk is getting me hungry. If you want to take out your favorite snack, now is a good time. My purpose for asking you all those questions is to get you to think about the experience that others have when they consume your personal brand.

When people come in contact with you they make a choice to consume or discard the product, "You." The taste of your personal brand is in essence the experience that others have from their interaction with you. Foods that don't taste good are usually discarded and foods that have great taste create an experience that allows them to be savored.

One of my favorite foods is the mango. I think it is one the greatest gifts we have on earth. When I eat a mango, it may take me thirty minutes or more because my experience is not to just eat it but to savor it. This means taking time to enjoy the aroma, peel the exterior skin, admire the green and red color, and enjoy the succulence of the juice surrounding the fruit. For me, the taste creates an experience that makes it one of my favorite foods. Now let's equate the concept of taste to your personal brand.

In building your personal brand, you want to create an experience with others that will keep them savoring you and the value you deliver. Thinking of yourself in this context will help you create the experience you want to leave with others. So here's your next assignment.

Step One: Assign yourself a taste

Step Two: Define the experience that others will have from their consumption of your personal brand

Step Three: Understand how your taste shapes your actions

For example, if I were a food product I would be a pineapple. My taste is sweet and the experience from consuming my personal brand is a sharp sweet delivery of substance. This understanding of taste and experience helps shape the conscious decisions, behaviors, and actions surrounding how I share my personal brand. It also helps me to consciously evaluate the feedback and perceptions of others and connect it with my personal view of myself to assess if I am delivering on my personal brand. So, for example, how does this sense of taste shape my actions?

Because I have a personal view of my "taste" as being a sharp, sweet delivery of substance, I am proactively and genuinely kind to others. I open doors and am the first one to offer my seat to a pregnant woman on a crowded subway train, I offer to stay late to help my team complete a project or wake up early to make sure my supervisor is prepared for his speech. I send notes to people who I have not spoken with in several months just checking to see if they are alive. These are just a set of actions among many that are shaped by how I believe I "taste."

Now it's your turn. Let's list your taste, experience, and actions below.

Taste—what type of food product would you be and why?
Experience—what is the experience that others get from consuming your personal brand?
Actions—what are your actions that are shaped by how you taste?

When you visualize this concept it spells TEA. So I guess you can say it's tea time.
Write down your taste, experience, and actions in the diagram below.

Taste	Experience	Actions

Now that you have completed this assignment, let's apply it to the Personal Brand Builder (PBB) below.

Brand Name	Style	Logo	Package	Mindset	Taste	Experience	Actions
Inspire	Sharp	Lightning bolt	Sharply dressed, well-groomed and tailored. Attention to detail with specific emphasis on color and contrast. Wardrobe conveys energy and radiance.	Always optimistic. Can do attitude at all costs. See the glass as half full. Seek to make a positive impact regardless of the circumstance. Brighten the outlook of others by accentuating positives and renouncing negatives.	Sweet Food product: Pineapple	Sharp sweet delivery of substance	Schedule ten minutes each day for some form of personal inspiration.
Happy	Bright	Sun	Bright colors that draw people in. Jewelry that stands out. A smile is an everyday accessory to your wardrobe.	Approach each day with a smile. Remain open to possibilities. See the glass as half full. Brighten the outlook of others by accentuating positives and renouncing negatives.	Sweet Food product: Ice cream	Always a treat Comforting and enjoyable	Pick flowers every day and set them by your desk.

Determi-ned	Bold	Hammer	Consis-tently dressed in dark, solid, bold colors with less use of pat-terns. Have one state-ment piece (jewelry, tie) that is a powerful identifier and says you are about busi-ness.	Thou-ghtful and focused. Seek reso-lution to conflict. Start each day with a goal and end with record of your achie-vement.	Neither sweet nor sour Food product: Red wine	Bold Full of subs-tance Com-plete	Make to-do lists and check them off as a sense of accom-plish-ment.
Outgoing	Casual and relaxed	Green grass	Anything goes. Dress according to how you feel that day. Prefer loose than form-fitting. Default to blue jeans or khakis whenever possible. Prefer but-ton down shirt or blouse to wearing a suit.	Go along with the flow. Accept that there will be ups and downs. Look to fit in as opposed to stand out. Receive opportu-nities that come your way but don't put too much pressure on yourself to create them.	Salty Food product Pop-corn	Happy and unpre-dictable Free spirited Life of the party Like to be among groups	Meet someone for a drink or conver-sation before heading home.
Your Brand Name	**Your Style**	**Your Logo**	**Your Pac-kage**	**Your Mindset**	**Your taste**	**Your expe-rience**	**Your Actions**

The taste of your personal brand and the experience you create with others will either support the value of your personal brand or quickly destroy its value. My goal is to get you to have the same response that Kellogg's Tony the Tiger has: "They're great!"

Category Versus Association

Assignment Number Six – Put yourself in a category and build your associations, affiliations, and circle of influence around it to support your personal brand.

There is a saying my mom and dad used to always recite to me. It says, "Show me who your friends are and I will know all about you." The affiliations you have, including your friends, your business circle, your community, and your family members have a direct correlation to your personal brand. Just like products on a shelf are put into a category to define their brand status. You will be perceived through the associations you have.

To effectively manage your personal brand, it is important to be conscious of the fact that others will perceive you and your value through the company you keep. So think of your circle, the people with whom you spend the most time, and the people who others associate you with as extensions of your personal brand. What this means is that if someone in your circle perhaps leaves a negative impression with others it potentially equates to you leaving that same negative impression which could ultimately limit the opportunities that come your way and devalue your personal brand. So here are some tips to help you focus on your brand associations.

Step One: Assign yourself a category

For example, are you a premium brand, an everyday brand, a household brand, a novelty brand, a vintage brand, or a brand with no associated name value? Having a predetermined category for how you associate yourself helps you to be directed to the things that are relevant to your brand and consistently support and define who you are.

For example, among the several brands of automobiles listed below, which one would you identify yourself with?

Ferrari ___ BMW___ Mercedes ___ Infinity___ Toyota___ Buick___ Saturn___

Your answer to this question may also signify the category you associate for your personal brand. In fact, an article titled "The Social Psychology of Driving" by Friedrich Nietzsche states that we should consider the extent to which one's sense of self is automotively linked. For some, you are what you drive. Here's an example to illustrate this point:

Brand of Automobile	**Personal Brand Attributes**
Ferrari	You look at yourself as a premium brand. You like the finest things, wear the finest clothes, and dine at the finest places. You place careful attention on who you are seen with publicly and look for opportunities to "be seen" by others in order to make an impression that elevates the perception of your worth.
BMW	You look at yourself as a superior performance brand. Not overly elite, but not casually ordinary. You want to stand out from a crowd, but want to do so by the things you accomplish which make you distinctly unique among others. You associate with others who have a similar ambition and drive toward superior performance.
Mercedes	You look at yourself as a classy brand that has a unique advantage over others. Class is important. You dress with class, entertain with a classy style, and view your surroundings as having a definite relationship to who you are. Your image is more important than your performance.
Infinity	You put yourself into a category signaling the middle of the pack. You are not overly concerned with image or being perceived as better than another person. You are also striving for a certain level of success that others see as strong ambition. Because you want to be better, others may see that as a sign that you will aspire to greater things in life and because of this you adapt to a variety of environments with no particular concern about the level of people in your surroundings or who you can impress.

Toyota	You see yourself as an everyday brand with an everyday attitude. You put yourself into the category that best fits your present situation and can adapt accordingly. You shy away from fancy occasions where class and elitism are more pronounced than fun and recreation. You associate yourself with people who just want to have fun and are not concerned with how they are perceived while having it.
Buick	You are a heritage brand and put yourself into a category of having prestige by virtue of how long you have been around and the wealth of your wisdom and your experiences. You often tell war stories as a way to engender community and bring people together. You are not concerned about portraying an elevated sense of self, but rather identify with others who can share experiences and wisdom.
Saturn	You put yourself into the category of a young upstart looking to take on the world by virtue of your youth and focus. You would rather be known as being efficient than being elite. You would also rather go the extra mile to show that you are capable than to tell others how great you are for them to grasp your value. You associate with any and everyone and consider yourself an average person with an average set of goals and dreams living an everyday lifestyle no different or worst than the person next to you.

The category you put yourself in will also shape your personal brand and help direct the perception you wish to create with others. If you have not given yourself a category, you may have already been put in one by those around you. So take notice of how you want to position yourself in the context of your surroundings and begin to live the category you want associated with your personal brand.

Step Two: Build your association and affiliations around the category you have identified for yourself.

To truly live the category you have identified for your personal brand, you must build associations that relate your brand to the people and things that define you. Companies like Procter & Gamble and Unilever have long built associate products alongside their core brands, also known as line extensions. Line extensions are defined as products that bear the same parent brand name and offer the consumer varied options. For example, a popular line extension is Diet Coke.

Brand line extensions are important because they allow a company to introduce new products, but reduce the risk of new product development because they can draw on the established success of the parent brand. When managed well, a line extension will not only make the new product successful, it will also promote the success of the parent brand.

If we relate this concept to your personal brand you will see that the associations that you build around you all have some relative value to promote or decrease the success of your personal brand. This includes the people who you work with, the people you socialize with, the organizations that you are a member of, the school or university you attended, the charities that you choose to donate to, the Web sites you choose to blog on, and the social networking sites you choose to join. Further, because these affiliations are associated to you, "the product," others will be more likely to associate themselves with your affiliations based on the perceived success of your personal brand.

The implications of this statement are that companies can promote their organization much more effectively through marketing their people than they can through general advertising and thus there is a quantifiable benefit to the value of personal branding across an enterprise. Likewise, as an established personal brand, you deliver much more value to your company than a less visible employee, thus you should be able to command a higher level of compensation.

Ad Age, the leading global source of news, intelligence, and conversation for marketing and media communities, reports that on average a thirty-second television spot will cost well over two hundred thousand dollars. The more targeted or vast the audience population that will be reached by the ad, the greater the premium on the cost to air a commercial. For example, it is well known that commercials during the Super Bowl command over a million dollars for a thirty-second spot. The reason this is important to address is that as a personal brand you must know that you are driving greater value for your life and for your affiliations.

In Chapter 1K I mentioned that as a personal brand you are giving over three thousand public announcements each day. If we were to quantify three thousand ads a day at two hundred thousand dollars an ad, you would derive at a number much greater than the average person's individual salary. My point is, while you may not make a six million dollar salary, if you are a well established personal brand you will be driving over six million dollars in brand value for your company, your affiliation, or just plainly for the value of your life. Conversely, if you have a negative personal brand, you may also be costing your company or association millions of dollars in reputation risk that will lead to your eventual demise or the demise of the things associated with you.

Building your personal brand is about building value for yourself and the people around you. People often say "I feel like a million bucks today!" What they are really saying is that I feel great about my personal brand. Think about the people and entities that you associate with and take an audit of your affiliations to ensure that they are delivering consistent attributes with the ones that will drive your success.

Performance Versus Impact

Assignment Number Seven - Identify your performance attributes

If you have ever bought a technology product or high-end appliance, you will know firsthand the importance of product performance. Products that perform well have greater impact and typically lead to future purchases of that same brand. For example, if you bought an Apple iPod and enjoyed its performance it would make you more likely to purchase an iPhone and related "i" accessories from this same brand. Managing your personal brand follows this same methodology. When you deliver high performance in whatever you do, it will lead to greater impact and influence others to select you for other opportunities. So the first thing you can do is to identify your performance attributes. By this I mean proactively identify three things you will do at a high level to create impact. This will help you formulate the capability attributes of your personal brand.

Step One: Identify your performance attributes
What are three things that you do well? Here's an example:

- I am a great communicator
- I am an avid reader
- I am a good leader

1. ______________________________

2. ______________________________

3. ______________________________

Step Two: Establish a plan for how you will create impact

After you have identified the things you do well, what will you do with your capabilities to create impact? Here's an example:

- I am a great communicator so I will create impact through public speaking.
- I am an avid reader so I will create impact by sharing information and little known facts to help others understand history.
- I am a good leader so I will create impact by volunteering to lead a challenging project or group.

Write what you will do to create impact

____

____

____

____

Step Three: Offer other personal brand accessories that others can buy

Now that you know what you do well, and how you will use your capabilities to create impact, what are other ways you can help others by using your talents? Here's an example:

- I am a great communicator, so I will create impact through public speaking. If you need someone to open up a meeting, introduce a speaker, be your keynote speaker, or make an announcement, I can help.
- I am an avid reader, so I will create impact by sharing information and little-known facts to help others understand history. If you need to create a trivia game for an ice breaker or are searching for the answer to a difficult trivia question, I can help.
- I am a good leader so I will create impact by volunteering to lead a project or group. If you need someone to take on a new assignment or relocate to another city to help a struggling division of the company, I can help.

What are the other personal brand accessories that others can buy from you?

___

___

___

___

Understanding the performance-impact ratio of your personal brand will give you a focused approach to ensure you are creating impact, not just delivering performance. The greater your ability to create impact the more your personal brand will resonate with others and create the demand for your personal brand accessories. Collectively this will allow your other attributes to shine.

Reviews Versus Reputation

Assignment Number Eight: Give yourself a product review to shape your reputation

Today, most consumers shop before they shop. The emergence of user review Web sites like Cnet.com, Consumerreports.org, and Epinions.com have empowered consumers to make the right product selection, pay the right price, shop at the right location, and weed out the products that are not worth considering. A product's review will establish its reputation and generate the word-of-mouth buzz that can drive its sales through the roof or put the product and its manufacturer out of business.

People also conduct people reviews and use the reputations of others to make the right people selection, weeding out those people who are not worth considering. To manage your personal brand effectively in the wake of people reviews, you must first give yourself a review. This can help shape the reputation you establish with others. Here are some tips for establishing a positive reputation.

Step One: Give yourself a product review

I'll admit it's easier to give someone else a product review than to give yourself one. But this is an important step in creating the reputation that others will use to make a decision on the purchase of your personal brand.

As discussed in Chapter 1K, by giving yourself a personal brand review, it demonstrates to others that you "know yourself" and have taken the time to assess your capabilities and your worth. This creates an impression in their minds that you have weeded out the attributes not worth considering and are presenting a fully confident and capable self. This outlook shapes your reputation and establishes the foundation for the word-of-mouth buzz that is generated for your personal brand. People believe in people who believe in themselves.

Here's a sample personal brand product review to illustrate this point.
Product: Personal Brand "Me"
User rating 9.0

My review
I am a solid leader capable of influencing others and delivering positive results. I work best when enabled to build a team to solve a clearly defined task and am focused on using facts to drive decision making. I am a passionate leader who leads by example and an innovator whose creativity takes whatever I am involved with to a new level of growth.

Your review
Product: Personal Brand "You"
User rating ?

Write your personal brand product review below.

____

____

____

____

When you give yourself a review, you are in a better position to evaluate if others have accurately captured your personal brand attributes. You are also able to see how you stack up to others when competing for the same goal or opportunity.

This approach is especially helpful when you are looking for a job or campaigning for a promotion. If people feel that you know yourself and understand that you have already given yourself a review they will spend more time trying to find proof to validate your review than they will trying to create a false review for you. As a result you will experience more positive outcomes.

Step Two: State the words you want associated with your reputation

After giving yourself a product review, identify the words you want to have used with your reputation. It is important to proactively select these words and not leave it up to others to assign them to you. When you have clearly established your reputation, you will actually begin to hear these same words when others describe you and when you are introduced to others. It's a great litmus test and when it works you will not be surprised at how others introduce you, because they will be using the same attributes as the ones you have already given yourself.

In Chapter 2K I mentioned the importance of "Knowing what you want to be known for." When you know what you want to be known for you will see that your personal product review and the user review given to you by others will have common themes and a consistent message. So list the words that you want associated with your personal brand. Here's an example:

- Great leader
- Reliable, can always count on him to get the job done
- Professional appearance and demeanor
- Inspires others, outstanding communicator, always delivers a quality presentation
- Very creative

What are the words that you want associated with your personal brand?

____

____

____

____

Step Three: Introduce yourself using the words you selected for your reputation

Now that you have given yourself a review and established the basis for your reputation, begin to incorporate this into how you introduce yourself to others. As stated in Chapter 2K, the way you introduce yourself has a significant impact on how you are perceived and thus on your personal brand.

This is especially true when meeting someone for the first time. The more you are able to use the words you want as the basis of your reputation, the more confident you will be in delivering this message and the impressions you want to convey as a result of it.

For example, I would say, "Hi, pleasure to meet you. I am Kaplan Mobray, the creative force behind this project," or "I am Kaplan Mobray, and I am looking forward to inspiring your people through my presentation." In this example I used the two words "creative" and "inspire" in my introduction. These are also words I used above in the reputation I wish to build with others. Inspire happens to also be my brand name.

So as you introduce yourself, make a conscious choice to use the words, phrases, and attributes that you associate with your personal brand. This will help you to become memorable and plant an early seed in the minds of others of who you are.

Advertising Versus Networking

Assignment Number Nine: Create your own advertising campaign and use it as a tool to network with others

Advertising is one of the most critical enablers of a product's success in the market. A good advertising campaign will generate recall of a brand and stimulate demand for the product. If you think about the ads displayed each year during the Super Bowl, they not only raise awareness of a product's brand but for almost every product advertised during the telecast there is a direct spike in sales following the airing of the ad. Further, the next day in offices and communities all across the country people have a conversation about the commercials, which establishes further recall of the product. Similarly, you will stimulate demand for your brand by having a well-executed advertising plan when networking with others. So here are some tips on creating your own personal brand advertising campaign.

Step One: Select three attributes that you will use to establish recall with those you meet.

In chapter 7K we discussed how you can make a connection just based on something distinguishable in your personal appearance. We also explored that you are able to affect strong recall for your personal brand by creating a unique experience that makes you stand out when you meet someone.

Some of the most memorable people brands have established themselves using this technique. For example, some choose a consistent style of dress, a notable demeanor, a memorable salutation or greeting, or distinct phrase or saying as the way that others will remember them and the way they will be portrayed in the media.

Here are some techniques celebrities have used to create their personal brand advertising campaign.

Celebrity	**Personal brand advertising campaign**
Michael Jackson	Wore a white glove when performing.
Donald Trump	Said the words "You're fired."
George Clooney	Became known for being a Hollywood hunk, and until recently never took a date to the Oscars.
Tiger Woods	Consistently wears a signature red shirt and black pants when competing on Sundays.
Ellen Degeneres	Always devotes the opening segment of her show to her dancing with the audience.
Latin music diva Celia Cruz	Always belted the word "azucar" in her performances.

If I were to cover up either side of this diagram, I bet you would still be able to quickly recall the celebrity that corresponds to the attribute.

What makes a personal brand advertising campaign effective is your ability to be consistent in what you do, say, wear, or think such that your behavior and actions are widely recognizable and expected by others. This is especially true in a networking situation or professional environment where you are looking to be recognized for your capabilities.

In chapter 3K I talked about the importance of being consistent as a way to build your personal brand. Further, I mentioned that as human beings we are taught to recognize patterns and sequences that we define and put into categories. When you create a consistent personal brand advertising campaign, you allow others to put you into a recognizable category that defines who you are and what others can always expect from you. As a result you become memorable.

So as you begin to create your personal brand, think about one action, one behavior, one signature personal appearance statement, or one specific other way that you can brand yourself in the minds of others. People remember people that make themselves memorable.

Step Two: Create your own ten-second elevator speech.

In chapter 5K we talked about the "elevator speech" and how it plays a role in helping you to deliver your value. An elevator pitch or speech is a well-practiced description about yourself or your company that anyone in any business should be able to understand in the time it would take to ride up an elevator. Whether it is six seconds, ten seconds, thirty seconds, or ninety seconds, what matters is that you are able to create personal or professional value from that encounter. As mentioned, an effective elevator speech should deliver the following three components.

a. A statement of who you are
b. A statement of what you are capable of delivering
c. A statement of how you can help others

Your elevator speech is your ticket to a ride to opportunity. Sometimes you do not need a lot of time to make yourself memorable, you just need a solid formula for engaging a conversation and communicating your value.

Step Three: Give yourself a slogan and develop a campaign-like focus for your personal brand.

In Chapter 7K we focused on engaging a conversation verbally, physically, and using signals like eye contact to establish a connection with others. In advertising, slogans are effective signals to hook consumers into remembering a product. When used well, slogans can actually take over the image of a product and thus the product recall in the minds of consumers is actually triggered by the slogan.

Let's take a walk down memory lane and see if you can guess the product behind these advertising slogans.

Slogan	Product/Brand
1. Where's the beef?	
2. Give it to Mikey, he'll eat anything	
3. Taste great, less filling	
4. We bring good things to life	
5. Zoom, zoom, zoom.	
6. They're magically delicious	
7. I'm lovin' it!	
8. Just do it	

9. It melts in your mouth, not in your hands.	
10. "Can you hear me now? Good."	

How did you do? I have listed the answers here so you can see your score. (1. Wendy's 2. Life Cereal 3. Miller Lite 4. General Electric 5. Mazda 6. Frosted Lucky Charms 7. McDonalds 8. Nike 9. M&Ms 10. Verizon)

Slogans bring back memories and whether you hear it for the first time, or hear it years from now they become an emotional way to remember a product. This same principle applies to building your personal brand.

People will create slogans for you without your knowing based on impressions that you make. For example, have you ever heard someone say "The Big Mouth is coming to the meeting." Or, "That person always has an opinion," or better yet, "She's angry." These are slogans that people use to describe others, sometimes in advance of them arriving to a room. They are also usually based on some kind of emotional response to that person that was established from negative impressions made in a previous encounter. The danger of having slogans assigned to you is that you, "the product," now become known based on your slogan. Just like in the advertising examples, people may only know you by your slogan and not by the capabilities that you can truly deliver.

When you have a focus on your personal brand, you want to create the slogans that people use to describe you. Specifically, you want to have an answer to the question we explored in chapter 5K. What do you want people to say about you the next day when you are not in the room? Here's an example:

"I want to be known as a sharp dresser who gets things done." I want people to say, "That guy is impressive." I want others to say, "That's the guy who plays a mean saxophone." I want others to use the slogan, "That's the 10K guy, he gives an awesome presentation." These are all slogans that I have predetermined that I want others to say about me when I am in or not in the room. Because I have a focus on the slogans that I want to precede me, "the product," I can focus on delivering the capabilities that make the slogans true. I do this, however, by creating an advertising campaign for my personal brand by sharing the attributes of my slogans with everyone I encounter.

So what is your slogan? And how will you use it to effectively signal the value of your product? Having a focus on your advertising campaign will help you create more meaningful connections and give you an approach to create greater recall of your brand.

Okay, I couldn't resist. Here are some more slogans. Can you match them with their products?

Slogan	Product/Brand
11. Good to the last drop	
12. The breakfast of champions	
13. Fly the friendly skies	
14. Finger-lickin' good	
15. The ultimate driving machine	
16. We try harder	
17. The quicker picker upper	
18. It's everywhere you want to be	
19. M'm! M'm! Good!	
20. The citi never sleeps	

Here are the answers: 11. Maxwell House Coffee 12. Wheaties 13. United Airlines 14. Kentucky Fried Chicken 15. BMW 16. Avis 17. Bounty 18. Visa 19. Campbell's Soup 20. Citibank

Durability Versus Consistency

Assignment Number Ten: Identify your most positive attributes and create specific actions that you will do consistently to promote them

Think for a second about batteries. Batteries are a common product, and in your lifetime you will most likely have had an experience using a product that requires batteries. You have either been very disappointed or pleasantly surprised at the product's durability. If you have been pleasantly surprised, it is because the battery's durability lasted longer than you expected and because of it you were able to enjoy and get greater use of the product. A product's durability can easily determine its worth. Similarly, the consistency of your personal brand will ultimately determine the value you have with others.

Earlier in this book we explored the 3rd K, "Know How to Be Consistent." We discussed the importance of consistently delivering your personal brand attributes and leaving a consistent impression with others. What enables you to be consistent is your ability to identify your most positive attributes. These are the qualities that create the strongest impression with others and make them an integral part of how you approach each day. Each of the elements in your Personal Brand Builder (PBB) should be consistent attributes that direct how you live and the impression you leave with others. So to put this into practice, define what you will do each day based on the attributes you have built for your brand through the Personal Brand Builder (PBB).

Step One: Identify your most positive attributes

For example:

a. Approachable
b. Talented
c. Creative

List your most positive attributes

a. ____________________

b. ____________________

c. ____________________

Step Two: Create specific actions that you will do to promote your positive attributes

For example:

a. Greet everyone with a smile
b. Offer a creative idea or approach to solutions
c. Participate in events that allow me to demonstrate my talents

What specific actions will you do as a result of your positive attributes?

a. ____

b. ____

c. ____

Conclusion

Personal branding is about promoting your most positive attributes so that you can create a favorable impression in the minds of others. It is important to have a specific set of actions that you do to establish your personal brand so that the impressions that you make are backed by facts. Let this section, the Personal Brand Builder, serve as a guide to help you calibrate your personal brand every day.

(K)atchup

In This Section

- Recap of 10Ks

Congratulations! You have just completed the 10Ks of Personal Branding. You are now equipped with the tools to begin your own personal brand journey. You will find many treasures along the way, but none greater than the personal and professional growth that you are about to experience. As we look back on what you have just accomplished, think about the brand called "YOU" and what you are going to do with the tools that you have just discovered.

In **Chapter 1K,** "**K**now Thyself," you gained an understanding of the importance of knowing yourself including your current strengths and how your past contributes to who you have become.

In **Chapter 2K,** "**K**now What You Want to Be Known For," you gave yourself a set of attributes that you want to be known for and laid the foundation for how you will be known by others.

In **Chapter 3K,** "**K**now How to Be Consistent," you confirmed your commitment to establish greater consistency between your personal and professional life.

In **Chapter 4K,** "**K**now How to Accept Failure as Part of Building Your Personal Brand," you reflected on your failures and the things that you have learned from your own experiences that have made you stronger, bolder, better, and more complete.

In **Chapter 5K,** "**K**now How to Communicate Your Personal Brand Attributes," you gained insight into the six-second elevator pitch and a view on what to communicate when trying to leave a memorable impression.

In **Chapter 6K,** "Know How to Create Your Own Opportunities," you explored strategies and methods to create opportunities that can change your life.

In **Chapter 7K,** "Know and Master the Art of Connection," you reflected on how you make connections with others and effective tips to use when networking.

In **Chapter 8K,** "Know That Silence is Not an Option," you focused on not being silent so you can create a memorable impression.

In **Chapter 9K,** "Know Your Expectations (Not Your Limitations)," you internalized the fact that if you don't expect much from yourself, and others don't expect much from you, then you will be limited from opportunities to advance in life.

In **Chapter 10K,** "Know Why You are Doing What You are Doing Today and How it Will Shape Where You are Headed Tomorrow," you started the process of personal brand planning so that you can begin to follow your dreams and pursue your goals.

In **Chapter Special K,** "Know How To Ask For What You Want," you gained an in-depth understanding of how to ask for what you want with an approach and style to ensure success.

In **Building Your Brand**, you were introduced to the Personal Brand Builder (PBB), a guide to help you understand how to apply the 10Ks in everyday living.

So there you have it: the 10Ks of Personal Branding

Use these principles to change your life, to give you focus, to propel your career, and to take yourself to a much greater place. In doing so, you will begin to see and experience dramatic results.

Life has an expiration date and although we don't know what date we are stamped with, we can manage the time we have to live life to the fullest. Don't allow the time that you have on this earth to go by without you asking for what you want and taking the actions you need to make them happen. Another way to put this is through my personal quote, "Life waits for no one so don't wait to live." Your personal brand is everything.

So here's my "ask." I ask you to share this book and these 10Ks of Personal Branding lessons with as many people as you can. There's a great life out there to be lived—start living yours today!

Thank you for reading the 10Ks of Personal Branding.

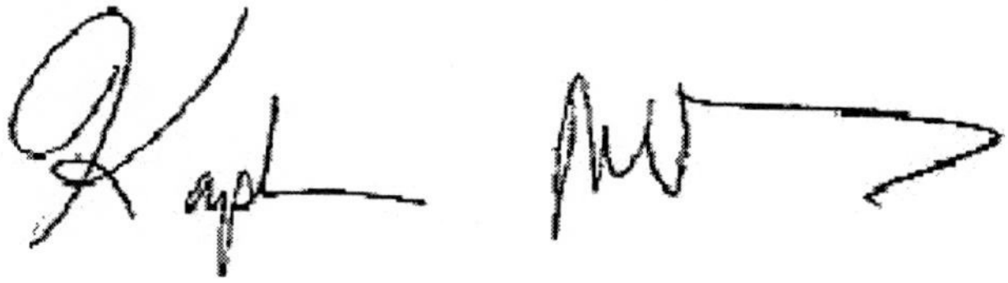

Kaplan Mobray

Bibliography

Academy of Achievement. "Julius Erving." http://www.achievement.org/autodoc/page/erv0bio-1

AdAge. http://www.adage.com (accessed October 1, 2007).

Answers.com. "Shirley Temple." www.answers.com/black-shirley-temple.

Athletes for Hope. "Lance Armstrong." http://www.athletesforhope.org/lancearmstrong.html.

Armour, Stephanie USA Today, " Working 9-to-5 No Longer. More Choose Flexible Hours on the Job." http://www.usatoday.com/educate/college/business/articles/20041212.htm

Balajadia, Dennis. "Is Brand Loyalty Dead?" http://www.brandchannel.com/view_comments.asp?dc_id=52 (posted January 5, 2005)

Brand Marketing and the Promotion Marketing Association. "Sampling is highly effective for marketers of consumer packaged goods." January 2001 https://www.pmalink.org/getPDF.asp?p=WhySamplingWhitePaper.pdf

Elsevier Science. "Keeping up one's appearance." Elsevier Science 2000 B.V. Schwer, Keith R. and Rennae Daneshvary. *Center for Business and Economic Research.* University of Nevada, Las Vegas, February 28, 2000.

Emmet, Teri. "The Psychology of being Organized." http://how-to-be-organized.info/the_psychology_of_being_organized.php (posted September 3, 2005)

Essortment. "Oprah Winfrey Biography." http://www.essortment.com/all/oprahwinfrey_rkcr.htm.

Fisk, Peter, *Marketing Genius.* Mankato: Capstone Publishing, 2006.

Garrett, Chris "Social media tools." www.chrisg.com.

Gitomer, Jeffrey. *The Little Red Book of Selling.* Bard Press, 2004.

Hall, Peter M. and Dee Ann Hall. "The Handshake as Interaction." *Semiotica* v.45. (1983): 249-264.

The Internet Movie Database. "Tom Hanks." http://www.imdb.com/name/nm0000158/.

Jacoby, Larry, Colleen Kelley. "Unconscious Influences of Memory for a Prior Event." *Personality and Social Psychology Bulletin*, Vol. 13, No. 3, 314-336 (1987).

Jobs DB Career Guide. "10 Steps to Pitch Yourself and Elevate Your Career." http://www.jobsdb.com (accessed August 5, 2008)

Khun, Maggie. "*When you least expect it, someone may actually listen to what you have to say.*" http://en.thinkexist.com/quotes/Maggie_Kuhn

LaFrance, Dr. Marianne. "The Study of First Impressions" http://www.lamasbeauty.com/beauty/september03/Impressions.htm (September 1, 2003).

Landy, David, and Harold Sigall. "Human Behavior Experiments: Judging a Book by Its Cover.. Beauty Is Talent: Task Evaluation as a Function of the Performer's Physical Attractiveness" in *Journal of Personality and Social Psychology*, Vol. 20, No. 3. (1974), 229-304
University of Rochester, Rochester, N.Y., 1972.

Liu, S.J., A.E. Katz " Success in the land of the Less" *Psychology Today*, Jan 1992 Article ID: 1949

Maslow, Abraham. Citation: Huitt, W. Maslow's hierarchy of needs 1954. *Educational Psychology Interactive*. Valdosta, GA: Valdosta State University. http://chiron.valdosta.edu/whuitt/col/regsys/maslow.html, 2004.

Mehrabian, A. "Communication Without Words" *Psychology Today*, 1968.

Middleton, David, and Steve Brown. *The Social Psychology of Experience.* Sage Publishing, 2005.

Mirrick, John. "William H Gates III: Before Microsoft." http://ei.cs.vt.edu/~history/Gates.Mirick.html.

Morgenstern, Stacy. "The Secret to Good Digestion." Divine Caroline. http://www.divinecaroline.com (accessed February 29, 2008).

Newspaper Association of America. "Not too long ago, the average American was exposed to over three thousand advertising messages in the average day." http://www.naa.org/display/retailheadlines/v1no4/pg6.html (accessed July 28, 2008)

Nietzsche, Friedrich. "The Social Psychology of Driving" *Sociological Forum*, 22, (2007) 4:474-498.

Paul, Anne Murphy. "A Different Tone of Voice." *Psychology Today* (Sep/Oct 1997): Article ID: 841.

Perry, Jack. *You're Fired: 66 Ways to Keep Your Job as a Sales Professional.* McKenna Publishing Group (January 15, 2005).

Quick MBA. "The Product Life Cycle." http://www.quickmba.com/marketing/product/lifecycle/.

Rank, Hugh, "How To Analyze Ads." *Persuasion Analysis by Professor Hugh Rank, http://webserve.govst.edu/pa/index.html* (accessed August 1 2008)

Schriffin, Deborah. "Handwork as Ceremony." *Semiotica* v.12 (1974): 189-202.

Seligman, Martin. "Positive Psychology, the study of optimal human functioning." *American Psychologist* (2000): 13, 25-28

Spear, Jane. *Gale Encyclopedia of Psychology*. Edited by Bonnie B. Strickland. Gale Group, 2nd ed., 2001.

Sunnafrank, Michael and Artemio Ramirez Jr., "At First Sight: Persistent Relational Effects of Get Acquainted Conversations." *Journal of Social and Personal Relationships, Vol.21, No. 3, 361-379 (2004).*

Tschohl, John. "The Power of Word-of-Mouth Advertising." The Canadian Management Institute. http://www.cim.ca/NResources/CanadianManager.asp (accessed July 29 2008)

US Department of Labor, "Nearly 29 million employees start their day between 4:30 am and 7:29am." US Department of Labor Research Library. http://www.usatoday.com/educate/college/business/articles/20041212.htm

23Jordan. "Michael Jordan's biography." www.23jordan.com/bio1.htm.

Endnotes

Chapter 1K

[1] Newspaper Association of America, "American Advertising in the Media," http://www.naa.org.

[2] Jane Spear, "The Key to Unlocking Consumer Psychology" in the *Gale Encyclopedia of Psychology*, 2nd Edition, edited by Bonnie B. Strickland (Gale Group, 2001).

[3] David Wallechinsky, Irving Wallace, and Amy Wallace, *The Book of Lists* (LB Books, April 1995).

Chapter 2K

[4] Stacy Morgenstern, "The Secret to Good Digestion," Divine Caroline, http://www.divinecaroline.com

Chapter 3K

[5] LaFrance, Dr. Marianne. "The Study of First Impressions" by Dr. Marianne LaFrance at Yale University. (September 1, 2003) http://www.lamasbeauty.com/beauty/september03/Impressions.htm

[6] Seligman, Martin. "Positive Psychology, the study of optimal human functioning," *American Psychologist* (2000).

Chapter 5K

[7] Jobs DB Career Guide, "10 Steps to Pitch Yourself and Elevate Your Career," http://www.jobsdb.com .

[8] Rank, Hugh, "How To Analyze Ads,",http://webserve.govst.edu/pa/index.html.

[9] Tschohl, John. "The Power of Word-of-Mouth Advertising," The Canadian Management Institute. http://www.cim.ca/NResources/CanadianManager.asp

Chapter 7K

[10] Peter M. Hall and Dee Ann Hall, "The Handshake as Interaction," *Semiotica*, v.45. (1983): 249-264.

[11] Deborah Schriffin, "Handwork as Ceremony," *Semiotica* v.12. (1974): 189-202.

[12] Anne Murphy Paul, "A Different Tone of Voice," *Psychology Today* (September/October 1997): Article ID: 841.

Special K

[13] Larry Jacoby and Colleen Kelley, *Personality and Social Psychology Bulletin*, Vol. 13, No. 3. (1987): 314-336.

Building Your Brand

[14] Nietzsche, Friedrich. "The Social Psychology of Driving 2007, Friedrich Nietzsche's Sociology,", *Sociological Forum*, 22, 4:474-498.

[15] AdAge, "Advertising Spend by Unit Measure 2008 Rate Card" http://www.adage.com (October 1, 2007).

CPSIA information can be obtained at www.ICGtesting.com
Printed in the USA
BVOW05s2257010216

435038BV00001B/1/P

9 780595 484812